Samuel Crumpe

An Essay on the Best Means of Providing Employment for the People

Samuel Crumpe

An Essay on the Best Means of Providing Employment for the People

ISBN/EAN: 9783744734813

Printed in Europe, USA, Canada, Australia, Japan

Cover: Foto ©Thomas Meinert / pixelio.de

More available books at **www.hansebooks.com**

AN ESSAY ON THE BEST MEANS OF PROVIDING EMPLOYMENT FOR THE PEOPLE.

TO WHICH WAS ADJUDGED

THE PRIZE

PROPOSED BY THE

ROYAL IRISH ACADEMY

FOR THE

BEST DISSERTATION ON THAT SUBJECT.

By SAMUEL CRUMPE, M. D.
M. R. I. A.

DUBLIN:

Printed by BONHAM. | Published by MERCIER & Co.

M. DCC. XCIII.

TO THE RIGHT HONOURABLE

JAMES EARL OF CHARLEMONT,

PRESIDENT OF THE ROYAL IRISH ACADEMY.

MY LORD,

VARIOUS are the motives which give birth to dedications. Thoſe which have occaſioned the following ariſe from the novel ſituation of the Author, and the nature of the performance he now ventures to make public.

A writer who, for the firſt time, expoſes his labours to general inſpection, will naturally ſeek protection from the man diſtinguiſhed by the acquiſitions of literature himſelf, and by the deſire and power of encouraging them in others. Should his Eſſays be in their nature political, and ſuch as involve the moſt material intereſts of ſociety, he may, without impropriety, expect the countenance of those distinguished by steady and genuine patriotism. Of this description are the pages which ensue; and so situated is the Author from whose pen they proceed. They, therefore, claim at once the patronage of the patriot and the man of letters. Obvious is the consequence. To your Lordship, as exhibiting the singular combination of such singular characters, they are respectfully inscribed: a tribute the more readily offered, as it cannot for a moment incur the most remote suspicion of self-interest, or the possible imputation of flattery.

I have the honour to remain,

MY LORD,

Your Lordship's most obedient,

Humble servant,

SAMUEL CRUMPE.

PREFACE.

A BRIEF ſtatement of the circumſtances which have given riſe to the compoſition and publication of the enſuing Eſſay, and of the principal objects the Author has therein held in view, may be neither unacceptable or unneceſſary to the reader.

On the 8th day of October 1791, the Royal Iriſh Academy received a letter, ſigned *A Friend to Ireland*, incloſing a Bank note for one hundred pounds, with directions that they ſhould immediately propoſe two prizes of fifty pounds each, one

one for the beſt eſſay on the *beſt Syſtem of National Education*, and the other for the beſt diſſertation on the ſubject of the enſuing pages. Of the comparative merit of the different Eſſays the Academy were themſelves to judge. The queſtions were accordingly made public, and, at the propoſed period, the prize for the beſt Eſſay on Education was adjudged to Doctor S. Dickſon; but as the different diſſertations on the ſecond ſubject were not deemed ſatisfactory, it was, on the 16th of June 1792, again propoſed for competition. The ſubſequent Eſſay was compoſed during the laſt four months of that year, and to it, after an examination of three others, the prize was adjudged on the 20th of April 1793. As it was too voluminous to be inſerted in the Tranſactions of the Academy, it is, with their approbation, now ſeparately offered to the public. By this, however,

it

it is not to be underſtood, that the Academy, as a body, adopt the different ſentiments and poſitions the work contains; in this particular it ſtands in the ſame predicament with the different articles which compoſe their Tranſactions, and reſpecting which it is declared, that "The "Academy, as a body, are not anſwer-"able for any opinion, repreſentation of "facts, or train of reaſoning, which "may appear in them; for which the "authors of the ſeveral eſſays are alone "reſponſible."

With reſpect to the execution of the work itſelf, a few obſervations ſtrike the Author as at preſent not inapplicable; and, firſt, as to the ſize of the performance;

It may be imagined that, in an attempt of this nature, all that was poſ-

ſible

ſible to be advanced in elucidation of the ſubject could be eaſily compriſed in a ſmaller ſpace; and that what might be condenſed into an eſſay has been expanded into a volume. Similar were the ſentiments of the Author at the commencement of his undertaking; and, engaged in the duties of a laborious profeſſion, ſo little is his portion of leiſure, that were he at firſt fully acquainted with the extent of the ſubject, the taſk would probably have by him been left unattempted: but its magnitude was not fully comprehended till the outlines were nearly traced, and partly filled up. So great, indeed, is the diverſity of matter, ſo extenſive and important the variety of objects which the examination of the queſtion unavoidably involves, that his conſtant aim has been to concentrate his obſervations, and abbreviate his diſcuſſions; and he is free to confeſs, that

the

the ſucceeding ſheets, even ſtill, appear to him rather as the ſkeleton of a work which might be compoſed on the ſubject, than as a full and perfect inveſtigation of its different parts and dependencies.

In peruſing the ſubſequent pages, the reader is not to expect entertainment from the beauties of ſtile, or ornaments of rhetoric; the work will only prove intereſting from any information it may convey. Its Author has avoided declamation; his ſubject precluded embelliſhment.

It may be imagined by ſome that the examination of the queſtion is in many places of too abſtract a nature; that the views of the writer ſhould have been more confined; and that his ſpeculations are frequently rather theoretical than practical.

tical. The views of the writer have been extenſive; he has not been very anxious to deſcend to very minute particulars, to recommend this favourite fabric, or that favourite bounty; to enter into the ſquabbles of intereſted competitors; or to calculate to a fraction what one manufacture coſts the country, or to a unit what number of labourers another employs. He has endeavoured to examine the queſtion from a more commanding eminence; to inveſtigate the *generally* operating defects and deficiencies which obſtruct occupation and induſtry; to comprehend the intereſt of *all* concerned; and to determine the beſt means of providing *general* employment for an *entire* people.

In treating of the different impediments to induſtry and labour, which have exiſted among different nations, the writer has adduced many inſtances from France;

and

and noticed, with ſatisfaction, their correction during the firſt revolution. Let not this be conſtrued into an approbation of the anarchy which has for ſome time ravaged that diſtracted country. The inſecurity of property which at preſent prevails among its miſerable natives, is alone ſufficient to annihilate induſtrious employment; is alone more deſtructive to every induſtrious principle, than all the inconveniencies of its ancient government combined.

In peruſing the Second Part, which was written laſt November, it will be perceived that ſome of the meaſures recommended have been carried into execution by our Parliament this ſeſſion. Many of their acts have, indeed, been peculiarly calculated to benefit the nation at large, and particularly to aſſiſt the lower claſs of the community. Yet,

ſtrange

ſtrange to tell! that claſs ſeem at preſent as much inclined to riot and diſorder as ever. From whatever cauſe theſe commotions proceed, they ſhould be inſtantly repreſſed by the ſtrong arm of power. The reformation of a mob ſhould never even be liſtened to, nor their aſſemblage be either countenanced or permitted. The author of this Eſſay will be found in ſeveral of its pages the advocate of the people; yet ſuch are his ſentiments, and ſuch muſt be thoſe of every ſubject who wiſhes to have any grievances that ſhall exiſt *conſtitutionally* and *peaceably* redreſſed.

The adjudication of a prize to one of its own members has been deemed by ſome a piece of indelicacy in any literary ſociety. But where they are numerous, to exclude all from competition would ſeem a meaſure ungracious at

once

once and injurious. Partiality can in ſuch caſes be always eaſily avoided. In the preſent inſtance it may not be amiſs to remark, that the Author had not the honour of a ſeat in the Academy at the time his Eſſay was adjudged the prize.

Limerick, Auguſt 1, 1793.

CONTENTS.

PART I.

On the best Means of providing Employment for civilized Man in general.

SECTION I.

On the beſt Means of introducing the Spirit of Induſtry and Labour among a People.

SECTION II.

On the principal Impediments to Induſtry and Labour which exiſt under different Forms of Government.

SECTION III.

On the Syſtem of Induſtry moſt beneficial to be purſued, and moſt productive of Employment to the People at large.

Further

PART

PART II.

SECTION I.

Of the Situation, general Productions, and Climate of Ireland.

SECTION

SECTION II.

Of the general Character, Habits, and Propensities of the People of Ireland.

SECTION III.

On the beſt Means of providing Employment for the People of Ireland.

§ 1.

§ I. Agriculture.

§ II.

§ II. Manufactures.

§ III.

§ III. Commerce.

What are the beſt Means of providing Employment for the People?

INTRODUCTION.

OF the infinite variety of ſubjects, which from the earlieſt ages have engaged the attention of mankind, the ſtudy of politics will be found upon conſideration, at once, the moſt momentous, and the moſt difficult. The importance of ſuch inquiries is ſo ſelf-evident, and univerſally acknowledged, as to require no elucidation; the ſources of that difficulty with which they are attended, may be eaſily and briefly explained.

If politics be conſidered as an *Art*, to be learned and purſued in a regular routine, fettered by precedent, and directed by example, maxims the moſt pernicious may be ſanctified and perpetuated; the errors of the darkeſt periods be tranſmitted to poſterity; and man experience the lapſe of ages, while the art of governing him well remains in a ſtate of infancy. If, on the other hand, politics be conſidered as a *Science*, the impediments which attend its ſtudy, appear equally difficult and neceſſary to be ſurmounted. In every ſcientific inquiry the neceſſity of deducing our concluſions from facts and experiments alone, has, by the immortal Bacon, been diſtinctly explained, and vigorouſly enforced; and ſince the publication of his writings, ſuch modes of inquiry have been ſucceſsfully extended to almoſt every department of knowledge. But with reſpect to *political* facts, the world ſeems yet too young to afford a ſufficiency for the foundation of axioms, univerſally juſt, or generally applicable. And with reſpect to experiments, where exiſts the genius capable of deviſing them? where lies the government by which they will be admitted? where the people among whom they may be tried with ſafety? The natural philoſopher, if he be not already ſupplied with facts, by which he may direct his reaſonings, or from which

which his conclusions may be deduced, can easily institute his experiments, with every prospect of enlarging the sphere of knowledge, and no possibility of disturbing his neighbour's felicity and repose. The philosopher in *politics* is neither gifted with such opportunities, nor, did such occur, could he pursue the necessary steps, without the risk of dangers the most serious and diffused. In his inquiries, therefore, he has principally to note the events which the histories of various nations offer to his view, the effects their different institutions have produced upon the people, and the variety of changes their several alterations have occasioned. Where such facts are deficient, or totally wanting, he can only be guided by reasoning; which, though frequently fallacious, is the only resource left; and he is therefore necessitated to canvas the merits of the mere opinions of his predecessors in the same labours; and to examine systems rather specious and attractive, than founded in solidity, or salutary if carried into execution.

The question proposed by the Academy, is a political one in the strictest acceptation of the term; and the more minutely it is confider-ed, the more evident will become its importance. That the morals and happinefs of a people de-pend, in a great degree, upon their being em-ployed in induftrious occupations, is an axiom that will not be controverted: that the wealth of kingdoms arifes not from the quantity of preci-ous metals they may poffefs, or from an ima-ginary balance of commerce in their favour, but from the quantity of productive labour exerted by its inhabitants, is a maxim which has been lately fully demonftrated; and that the populouf-nefs, and ftrength of a nation, are proportioned to the numbers employed in active purfuits, is a principle which will be univerfally admitted. On the employment of the people, therefore, depend their own felicity and wealth, their con-ftitution's permanency and vigour; and to deve-lope the beft means of providing fuch employ-ment, is a tafk of the laft, and moft extenfive importance.

The obftacles with which the execution of fuch an attempt is attended, are indeed confider-able, and might be minutely detailed; but the present prefent is not a place for fuch an enumeration; the attempt is made, and the degree of fuccefs will be appreciated, not by the difficulties, but by the merits of the performance.

Previous to a more intimate difcuffion of the queftion propofed, it feems neceffary to afcertain with every poffible degree of accuracy, the precife meaning of the terms in which it is conveyed. Its general import is fufficiently obvious; but with refpect to the fenfe intended to be annexed to the word *People*, the author of the prefent effay feels in fome degree dubious.

On the moft fuperficial confideration it will appear evident, that the beft means of providing employment for the people, muft vary, not only in every kingdom, but in every diftrict of the fame kingdom. The difference of climate, foil, fituation, and natural productions; the diverfity of national or even provincial character; the different degrees of civilization, induftry, or refinement which already prevail;—thefe, and a thoufand other caufes, muft neceffarily occafion the variation alluded to. If, therefore, by the word

people

people be underſtood the *Iriſh People*, as the ſituation, title, and general views of the Academy would lead us to ſuppoſe, the Eſſayiſt is to concentrate his views on that nation, and to examine the nature of its productions, the general habits of its natives, the improvements they have already introduced, and thoſe which may be eſtabliſhed to the advancement of induſtry and encouragement of labour.

If, on the contrary, the term *people* be taken in a more extended ſenſe, and that it is intended to inveſtigate, what, *in general*, are the beſt modes of providing employment for civilized mankind; the remarks of the inquirer muſt be more univerſally applicable, his obſervations deduced from more widely operating cauſes, and his reaſonings and concluſions be rather general than appropriate.

Notwithſtanding, however, that the propriety of the diſtinction juſt laid down, cannot well be controverted, it muſt at the ſame time be admitted, that many principles may be diſcovered, from a *general* ſurvey of the ſubject, which will apply

apply to almoſt every particular nation. And as the importance of any concluſions to be formed from the examination of the queſtion before us, muſt be proportioned to the extent of their application; as an acquaintance with the ſubject in *general* will enable us the better to underſtand the intereſts of any nation in *particular*; and as it is the deſire of the Eſſayiſt to diſcuſs every topic which *might* have been intended to be conveyed by the queſtion, he ſhall divide the ſubject into two parts, and, in the firſt, attempt to inveſtigate, what are the beſt means of providing employment for the people in general of *any* civilized ſtate. In the ſecond, he ſhall endeavour to determine which are particularly applicable to the people of *Ireland*, and what modes may, in their preſent ſituation, be recurred to, with the greateſt proſpect of ſucceſs.

PART I.

General reflections—Motives productive of labour —Indolence of savages—Additional motives to labour which result from civilization—Two general causes of labour—General division of the subject.

THERE is no branch of philosophy, which has been cultivated with less success, than that which professes to analyze and explain the different tendencies and operations of the human mind. Nor is there any attempt in politics, more difficult to be executed, than an endeavour to alter the general character, habits, and propensities of a people.

These two reflections obviously occur, at the very commencement of the present discussion. For

For in endeavouring to aſcertain the beſt modes of providing employment for man, and of rendering the individual induſtrious, it ſeems neceſſary in the very firſt inſtance to determine, what are the movements of the mind which principally rouſe him to labour and exertion, and what are the moſt efficacious means of exciting a ſpirit of induſtry and labour in a nation in general. An inſight into the firſt of theſe points, will enable us to direct with ſome advantage our inquiries reſpecting the ſecond; of which as clear and comprehenſive a knowledge as poſſible ſeems materially, nay, abſolutely neceſſary. It is uſeleſs to furniſh a people with the means and materials of employment, if they will *not* be employed. It is vain to offer the inſtruments and rewards of labour, if they be neglected or refuſed.

If we look round the animal world, it will be clearly perceived, that there prevails in every ſpecies a natural averſion to labour: that each individual of them, is in general merely rouſed into temporary exertion by ſome preſſing deſire; and that as ſoon as ſuch is ſatisfied, they re-

lapſe

lapſe again into indolence and repoſe. Man, ſo far partakes of the nature of the mere animal in this inſtance, when unpoliſhed and uninfluenced by the effects of aſſociation and civilization, that his exertions will be found confined to the gratification of his mere ſenſual deſires, his labour, to the ſatisfying temporal, and preſſing neceſſities. “ The people of the “ ſeveral tribes of America,” ſays Robertſon, “ waſte their life in a liſtleſs indolence. To be “ free from occupation ſeems to be all the en- “ joyment towards which they aſpire. They will “ continue whole days ſtretched out in their “ hammocks, or ſeated on the earth, in perfect “ idleneſs, without changing their poſture, or “ raiſing their eyes from the ground, or utter- “ ing a ſingle word. Such is their averſion to “ labour, that neither the hope of future good, “ nor the apprehenſion of future evil, can ſur- “ mount it. They appear equally indifferent to “ both, diſcovering little ſolicitude, and taking “ no precautions, to avoid the one, or to ſecure “ the other. The cravings of hunger may rouſe “ them, but as they devour with little diſtinc- “ tion, whatever will appeaſe its inſtinctive de-

" mands, the exertions which these occasion are " of short duration. Destitute of ardour, as well " as variety of desire, they feel not the force " of those powerful springs, which give vigour to " the movements of the mind, and urge the " patient hand of industry to persevere in its " efforts."

Of the desires of mankind in a state of barbarism, the most powerful is the appetite of food; of his necessities, the most pressing is that of defence from the inclemency of seasons. As long therefore as man remains in a state approaching that of nature, his industry, and the quantity of labour he exerts, will probably be proportionate to the difficulties he has to encounter in satisfying these necessary wants; and hence they will be generally least in the most fertile soils, and the most temperate climates. On this principle perhaps there may be some slight foundation for the observation of those writers, who remark that the most industrious nations have in general been those which laboured under the greatest natural disadvantages.

But in civilized ſociety, man is rouſed into activity, and prompted to induſtry, by many additional and powerful motives. His acquired appetites and deſires become equally numerous, and importunate; and although the demands of nature ſhould be ſatisfied, he is ſtill ſtimulated to labour and induſtry, by thoſe artificial wants, which civilization has introduced, and cuſtom and example have rendered neceſſary. Such acquired motives are even more powerful than thoſe ariſing from the mere neceſſities of nature. The latter are, comparatively ſpeaking, eaſily gratified; the operation of the former is conſtantly felt, and conſtantly increaſing. "Le "travail de la faim," as Raynal finely obſerves, "eſt toujours borné comme elle, mais le tra-"vail de l'ambition croit avec ce vice même."

Two cauſes therefore exiſt, which principally rouſe man from that indolence and inactivity, to which he is naturally prone. Firſt, the original neceſſity of food and raiment; and ſecondly, the deſire of enjoying the comforts and conveniencies introduced by civilization.—And from this brief and abſtract, but neceſſary in-

quiry

quiry refpecting them, one might at firft view be inclined to conclude, that to anfwer the queftion propofed by the Academy, it would be almoft only neceffary to develope the means by which a tafte for the comforts and conveniencies of life could be beft introduced, and moft univerfally diffufed among a people. For as fuch taftes and defires muft be confidered the principal incentives to affiduous, induftrious, and fyftematic labour, where their operation is felt, their effects, it may be fuppofed, muft neceffarily follow.

To devife and explain the beft means of introducing fuch a tafte, is indeed a leading, and neceffary ftep. But it is not the only one requifite in the prefent undertaking. Other caufes tend, though not perhaps fo forcibly, to excite a fpirit of induftry and labour, which muft alfo be noticed. Befides,

Man has in no civilized community been fuffered to exert or direct his labour, and induftry, unfettered and unreftrained. Oppreffive laws, impertinent reftrictions, and unwholefome regulations,

lations, have palsied his arm, and curbed or totally suppressed his activity. To detect and elucidate the injurious tendency, and impolicy, of such impediments, is therefore another necessary and important division of our essay.

Supposing even man enjoyed the most unlimited liberty, in directing his activity and exertions, such are the mistakes to which he is naturally exposed, that passion, prejudice, or erroneous reasoning, may prompt him to pursue and persist in some modes of labour and industry preferably to others more beneficial to himself, and more productive of useful employment to his fellow citizens. To determine therefore in general, the most beneficial channels to which the labour and industry of a people should be principally directed, becomes a third necessary branch of the proposed subject. And if the question be considered in a general point of view, as is our intention in the present part of our essay, these three divisions appear to comprehend the whole of what can be advanced towards its elucidation. I shall, therefore,

Firſt, Endeavour to point out the beſt means of introducing and generally diffuſing among a people, a ſpirit of induſtry and labour.

Secondly, I ſhall attempt to diſcover, what are the principal impediments to induſtry and labour, which different forms of government, and various reſtrictions and regulations, have occaſioned. And,

Thirdly, I ſhall endeavour to ſhew, what is in general the ſyſtem of induſtry the moſt beneficial to be purſued, and the moſt productive of employment to the people at large.

SECTION I.

On the beſt Means of introducing the Spirit of Induſtry and Labour among a People.

Difficulty of altering national habits—Imitative propenſity of man—Neceſſaries of life, what—Divided into artificial and natural—The paſſion for artificial neceſſaries a great ſource of induſtry—Example of this—Three circumſtances requiſite to render the taſte for artificial neceſſaries the means of making man induſtrious—1ſt, The general diffuſion of an example—2dly, The object of imitation muſt not greatly exceed thoſe already enjoyed—3dly, Labour ſhould be neceſſary to the acquiſition of the propoſed object, and when exerted ſhould never be ineffectual—Proofs of this, from the conduct of thoſe who for ſlight ſervices receive exorbitant wages—from the effects of the Engliſh poor laws—Still the liberal reward of labour promotes induſtry—Partial exceptions to this maxim—Its general juſtice enforced—Arguments in oppoſition to this maxim

 refuted

refuted—Further proof of the justice of this general maxim—The reward of labour may be nominally high and really low—Taxes on necessaries produce this effect—Other injuries they occasion—Other expedients for making a people industrious—Employment of capital—Power of general example—Correction of vices destructive of industry—Drunkenness—A proper and universal system of education—Encouragement to particular branches of industry—Concluding considerations.

SECTION I.

AN attempt of greater difficulty, as was before obſerved, can ſcarcely be deviſed, than that of altering the general character and habits of a people. To counteract the propenſities of an individual, even before they are confirmed by habit, requires the moſt unremitting attention, the moſt prudent exertion of parental authority. How much more arduous the taſk, where no ſuch authority is poſſeſſed, where ſuch habits are confirmed, and where the change is to be effected among millions? The legiſlature of a nation may, by its edicts and authority, prevent the commiſſion of crimes; but ſhould it interfere in thoſe concerns, in which every individual muſt naturally be ſuppoſed more intereſted, than the members of that government under which he lives; ſhould it endeavour to compel a people to induſtrious purſuits or to a preference of particular branches of induſtry, ſuch attempts will be either impotent, or ruinous and oppreſſive. Changes of this nature can never be either forced, or ſuddenly effected.

Their introduction muſt be mild, their progreſs gradual. As compulſion, therefore, cannot be employed with any proſpect of ſucceſs in exciting a ſpirit of induſtry, to what expedient are we to have recourſe? Principally, I believe, to the influence of *Example*. I here take the word in a very comprehenſive ſenſe, as will ſoon be obvious.

Man is by nature a being of a very imitative nature; he is alſo univerſally actuated with the uſeful ambition and deſire of enjoying the various comforts and conveniencies, which his neighbours poſſeſs; and hence, as we have already noticed, a taſte for ſuch comforts and conveniencies is one of the great ſources of labour and induſtry. Some of the acquired wants of this nature become, in effect, neceſſaries of life, by the prevalence of cuſtom and example; others may be more properly termed luxuries. The nature of each is very well defined by that celebrated writer Dr. A. Smith, whoſe treatiſe, On the Wealth of Nations, is an invaluable fund of political knowledge; and whoſe ſentiments we ſhall have frequent occaſion to

recur

recur to in the prefent effay. “ By neceffaries,” fays he, “ I underftand, not only the commo-“ dities which are indifpenfably neceffary for “ the fupport of life, but whatever the cuftom “ of the country renders it indecent for cre-“ ditable people, even of the loweft order, to “ be without. The Greeks and Romans lived, “ I fuppofe very comfortably, though they had “ no linen. But in the prefent times, through “ the greater part of Europe, a creditable day-“ labourer would be afhamed to appear in pub-“ lic without a linen fhirt; the want of which “ would be fuppofed to denote that difgrace-“ ful degree of poverty, which it is prefumed “ nobody can well fall into without extreme “ bad conduct. Cuftom, in the fame manner, “ has rendered leather fhoes a neceffary of life “ in England. The pooreft creditable perfon, “ of either fex, would be afhamed to appear “ in public without them. In Scotland, cuftom “ has rendered them a neceffary of life to the “ loweft order of men, but not to the fame order “ of women, who may, without any difcredit, “ walk about barefooted. In France, they are “ neceffaries neither to men, nor to women; the

“ loweft

" loweſt rank of both ſexes appearing there
" publickly, without any diſcredit, ſometimes
" with wooden ſhoes, and ſometimes barefoot-
" ed. Under neceſſaries, therefore, I compre-
" hend, not only thoſe things which nature,
" but thoſe things which the eſtabliſhed rules
" of decency, have rendered neceſſary to the
" loweſt rank of the people."

Such comforts and conveniencies as Dr. Smith deſcribes, may, I think, be termed the *artificial neceſſaries* of life; the articles of mere ſubſiſtence may be called *abſolute* or *natural neceſſaries:* And if it be recollected, that when civilization is ſomewhat advanced, the exertion of one man is ſufficient to provide food for a great many, and that therefore the labour of a few would be ſufficient to ſupport the majority, it will be allowed, that man muſt neceſſarily remain in a comparative ſtate of inactivity, did he feel no other incentive to labour than the want of abſolute and natural neceſſaries. But different conveniencies, and various articles of cloathing, lodging, furniture, and ornament, are gradually invented and aſpired after. Each man labours

either

either to gratify himſelf with them, or to ſupply his richer neighbour, from whom, in return, he derives the means of furniſhing himſelf with the abſolute neceſſaries, and the inferior and more common comforts of life. In order to procure theſe latter, the working and poorer orders emulate each other, in the cheapneſs and elegance of their ſeveral productions. Induſtry, invention, and labour, are ſeverally employed, in the collection and improvement of rude materials. The huſbandman is rouſed to ſupply the artiſt with food, in order to receive in return a portion of his manufactures. And thus the vanity, taſte, and ambition of man, become the ſprings of labour and induſtry, and the ſource of uſeful employment. The quantity of labour, which the gratification of theſe deſires ſets in motion, is much more conſiderable than can at firſt view be imagined. The woollen coat, for example, which covers the day labourer, is, as Smith obſerves, the produce of the joint labour of a multitude of workmen. The ſhepherd, the ſorter of wool, the comber, the dyer, the ſpinner, the weaver, the fuller, the dreſſer, all join their different arts. How many merchants

merchants and carriers befides muft have been employed in tranfporting the materials from fome of thefe workmen to others? How many fhip-builders, failors, fail and rope makers, muft have been employed to bring the different drugs made ufe of by the dyer? What variety of labour is neceffary to produce the tools of the meaneft of thefe workmen? To fay nothing of the fhip, the fulling-mill, or even the loom, what variety of labour is neceffary to form even the fhears of the clipper? the miner, the builder of the furnace, the feller of timber, the burner of charcoal, the brick-maker, the brick-layer, the mill-wright, the forger, the fmith, all join their different arts in order to produce them.

From thefe fimple confiderations it will appear fufficiently evident, that a certain degree of tafte for the neceffaries of life, as above defined, muft be generally felt by a people before they can become induftrious. And wherever fuch defires are ftrongly felt, and generally diffufed, and the means of gratifying them known, and within reach, a people fo circumftanced and actuated, if not prevented by op-

preffion,

preſſion, ill-deviſed regulations, or other counteracting cauſes, will neceſſarily become active, induſtrious, and laborious.

As an example and illuſtration of what has been advanced, I cannot avoid inſerting a genuine and natural little anecdote, related by the celebrated Dr. Franklin. " The ſkipper," ſays he, " of a ſhallop employed between Cape May " and Philadelphia, had done us ſome ſmall " ſervice, for which he refuſed to be paid. " My wife, underſtanding that he had a daugh" ter, ſent her a preſent of a new-faſhioned cap. " Three years after, this ſkipper, being at my " houſe, with an old farmer of Cape May his " paſſenger, he mentioned the cap, and how " much his daughter had been pleaſed with it. " But, ſaid he, it proved a dear cap to our " congregation.—How ſo ?—When my daughter " appeared with it at meeting, it was ſo much " admired that all the girls reſolved to get " ſuch caps from Philadelphia, and my wife " and I computed that the whole could not have " coſt leſs than an hundred pounds. True, " ſaid the farmer, but you don't tell all the

" ſtory.

"ſtory. I think the cap was, nevertheleſs, an "advantage to us; for it was the firſt thing "that put our girls upon knitting worſted mit- "tens for ſale at Philadelphia, that they might "have wherewithal to buy caps and ribbons "there. And you know that that induſtry has "continued, and is likely to continue, and en- "creaſe to a much greater value, and anſwer "better purpoſes."

In order to derive any advantage from the deſire of enjoying the artificial neceſſaries of life, and the imitative propenſities of man, and to make them the means of rendering him induſtrious, three circumſtances ſeem materially requiſite.—The example to be imitated muſt be pretty generally diffuſed among a people. The object it propoſes muſt not be conſiderably above thoſe already enjoyed. And, to acquire it, although labour and induſtry ſhould be neceſſary, they ſhould never be vain and ineffectual.

Why the general diffuſion of an example is neceſſary to its univerſal adoption, ſeems eaſily explicable.

explicable. One powerful ſource of the deſire of enjoying the conveniencies of life, is that the want of them is uncreditable, and attended with a certain degree of diſgrace. But where a conſiderable number ſubmit to, and experience ſuch wants, the diſcredit, as in other inſtances, becomes as it were divided between them; each contentedly bears his own ſhare, and ſheltering himſelf under the example of the many, averts or mitigates the diſgrace, to the full force of which he muſt be expoſed, were his ſituation uncommon, peculiar, or ſolitary.

To perſuade all the inhabitants of a wretchedly built village to form more comfortable and commodious habitations, it is not ſufficient that one, or a few of them, ſhould in that reſpect conſiderably better their ſituation. Each of the remaining majority ſees that his neighbours contentedly inhabit their old huts. Why ſhould he not bear the ſame inconveniencies? They countenance his indolence, he feels no diſcredit from his ſituation, and the example, being partial, is nearly uſeleſs.

We

We may hence derive the reaſon of the inutility of thoſe ſmall colonies which have been planted in many countries emerging from barbarity, deſolation, or indolence, as examples to actuate their inhabitants to induſtry and labour. Such were in general the families introduced into Ireland from Germany, under the name of *Palatines*, and planted up and down in different counties. They were more induſtrious, laborious, and frugal, and conſequently better fed, and more comfortably lodged, than the generality of the labouring natives; but their mode of life, being confined to a few, was never imitated by their neighbours. And if the inhabitants of ſeveral diſtricts of the country are at preſent as laborious, and live as comfortably as the foreigners then propoſed to their imitation, it is to be aſcribed, not to the influence of their example, but to changes induced among the people at large. Were the intereſt and improvement of the natives, the only motives for the plantation of theſe colonies, ſuch views would have been much more effectually anſwered by a proper management of the people themſelves.

To derive any advantage from the ambition and imitative propenſity of man, it is equally neceſſary, that the improvement, and object of imitation propoſed, ſhould not greatly exceed thoſe he already enjoys. Where the difference in this reſpect is very conſiderable, ſo ſtrong is the averſion of the human race to any violent and ſudden alteration in the modes of life, that any attempt at introducing ſuch, ſeems rather to produce an oppoſite effect, and to confirm a people in their original barbarity and miſery. The free ſavages of America do not appear to have made the ſmalleſt progreſs in civilization ſince the ſettlement of the Europeans among them. Their improvement, in this reſpect, would have probably been much more conſiderable, had they been left to themſelves. Civilization and general aſſociation were commencing, as it were, in two points, among them, in the kingdoms of Peru and Mexico. They would probably have diverged from theſe centres in every direction; and as their improvements and alterations muſt neceſſarily have been ſlight and gradual, they would have been more eaſily and univerſally adopted, and in the end tended more to have meliorated their condition, than the arts, manners, and civilization of Europe, which being confiderably fuperior to any they were acquainted with, have been generally viewed with neglect or averfion. From fimilar principles, we may expect the fame effects in New Holland. The plantation of our colonies in that country, inftead of civilizing its favage natives, may but confirm them more ftrongly in their original barbarity.

Even in thofe countries where civilization has made confiderable progrefs among their inhabitants, the fame averfion to fudden and great changes is eafily difcernible. The progrefs of man in improvement muft be gradual, and every alteration and advantage offered to his acceptance muft be proportioned to thofe he is already in poffeffion of, which they fhould not vary from or exceed in any very confiderable degree. The glare of fun-fhine, which will affift the eye if progreffively introduced, will, if fuddenly admitted, but dazzle and confound our vifion. The fummit of civilization may be attained, by *gradually* advancing from ftep to ftep; but

but any attempt to elevate man at *once* to ſuch an eminence, will ever prove fruitleſs or injurious.

To render the ambition and imitative propenſity of man the means of making him induſtrious and laborious, it is, in the third place, requiſite, that labour and induſtry ſhould be neceſſary to the acquiſition of the prizes they propoſe, and that ſuch labour and induſtry ſhould never be ill rewarded, fruitleſs, and ineffectual. —" Ce n'eſt pas aſſez," ſays Rouſſeau, " d'a-" voir des citoyens, & de les protéger; Il faut " encore ſonger à leur ſubſiſtence. Ce devoir " n'eſt pas comme on doit le ſentir, de rem-" plir les greniers des particuliers, & es diſpen-" ſer du travail; mais de maintenir l'abondance " tellement à leur portée, que pour l'acquerir " le travail ſoit toujours néceſſaire, & ne ſoit " jamais inutile."—The maxim, here confined to the abſolute neceſſaries, may be with equal juſtice extended to the comforts and conveniencies of life.

The

The neceſſity of rendering labour and exertion inevitable requiſites to the acquiſition of theſe neceſſaries, if our intention be, to make man's paſſion for enjoying them one of the expedients for rendering him induſtrious, would ſeem to require but little illuſtration; a few proofs, however, will explain the general doctrine, and confirm its juſtice and importance.

It is a natural principle in the human race to appreciate the value of every acquiſition by the degree of difficulty neceſſary to its attainment. The workman, therefore, who receives but the uſual and proportionate reward for his exertions, is the moſt apt to employ any ſurplus that remains, after ſupplying his abſolute neceſſities, as a capital towards encreaſing his little ſtock, and ſetting a ſtill greater quantity of labour in motion for his further emolument. On the contrary, thoſe who, by ſlight, temporary exertions, receive rewards or wages diſproportionate to their labour, and extravagantly high, in place of encreaſing ſuch exertions, and employing their gains in induſtrious purſuits, will generally be found indigent, idle, and diſſolute,

and

and ever ſquandering their wages as lightly, as they were eaſily acquired. Of ſuch we have numerous inſtances in the various attendants upon young men of fortune and extravagance, and the crowds who reſort for employment to the different places of public amuſement and profuſion. This deſcription of people in general receive much higher rewards for their ſlight and eaſily effected ſervices, than the labouring workman, ingenious mechanic, or induſtrious manufacturer; yet where ſhall we find an aſſemblage more indolent, extravagant, or depraved? From the ſame principle does it in a great degree proceed, that cities reſorted to by the higher claſſes of ſociety, and where conſequently a great quantity of money is annually ſpent in prodigal profuſion, are generally very diſadvantageous ſituations for manufactures, or any employment which requires the regular exertion of induſtrious labour. "In mercantile and manufacturing "towns," ſays Smith, "where the inferior ranks "of the people are chiefly maintained by the "employment of capital, they are in general in-"duſtrious, ſober, and thriving, as in many Eng-"liſh, and in moſt Dutch towns. In thoſe towns

" which are principally ſupported by the conſtant, " or occaſional reſidence of a court, and in " which the inferior ranks of people are chiefly " maintained by the ſpending of revenue, they " are in general idle, diſſolute, and poor, as " at Rome, Verſailles, Compiegne, and Fon- " tainbleau." To the liſt we may ſurely add Dublin. I know not a more diſadvantageous ſituation for any undertaking than the idle and diſſipated capital of a country, in which idleneſs and diſſipation are ſtill too predominant; and the effects of ſuch a ſituation are but too viſible, in the riots and clamours of its diſſolute and ſtarving manufacturers.

From the ſame principles we may derive the reaſon, why an induſtrious village has been ſometimes obſerved to grow idle, on a wealthy lord's fixing his reſidence near it. The unuſual flow, and unequal diſtribution of money among its inhabitants, poiſons that induſtrious principle, which a more ſcanty and better proportioned ſupply, had given birth to, nouriſhed, and rendered flouriſhing.

The operation of a ſimilar cauſe is exemplified, and its baneful conſequences too fully proved, in the hiſtory of the effects of the poor laws of England. The injuries they otherwiſe occaſion, we ſhall have opportunities to touch on hereafter ; at preſent we have only to notice their tendency to repreſs induſtry, and encourage indolence.

It has juſt now been ſhewn, that great and diſproportionate rewards, for ſlight and temporary exertions of labour, inſtead of rendering thoſe who receive them induſtrious and laborious, produce an oppoſite effect, and prove a certain encouragement to indolence and depravity. How much more certainly muſt an inſtitution produce ſimilar effects, which holds out as it were a premium to idleneſs ; which ſupplies with food, clothing, and medicine, the indolent wretch who will not work at all ; and which levies ſuch ſupplies on the induſtry of his laborious neighbours. The Engliſh writers on this inſtitution, give but too ſtriking proofs of the various injuries it occaſions. Doctor Davenant aſſerts, that the poor rates of England will ultimately ruin

 her

her manufactures; and computes, that those who subsist on them amount to one million two hundred thousand, of whom at least one half would have persisted in the paths of industry and labour, if not seduced from them by the prospect of indolent subsistence on parish charity. The enormity and pressure of the poor rates, has at length roused the inhabitants of some parts of England to a sense of the mischiefs their application has occasioned, and continues to produce; and they have been led to exchange the usual mode, for the establishment of receptacles, which *really* deserve the name of *Houses of Industry*. This has been particularly effected at Shrewsbury, and an account of the undertaking has been published, which well deserves perusal and attention. From the introduction of the sensible and benevolent author of this pamphlet I shall select the following passages, which will strongly tend to confirm the opinions which have been advanced. "It is too evident, that "while the poor are supported in idleness, they "will be averse to labour, and the indolence "thus encouraged, is the fruitful parent of that "debauchery and depravity, and that consequent "wretchedness

"wretchedneſs and miſery, which have made ſo "fatal a progreſs among the lower orders of "the community. Every caution will be re- "laxed, and every profligacy indulged, by men "ſo diſpoſed, from the conſideration that nei- "ther themſelves nor their families can ever "ſtarve—Whilſt they can have their wants ſup- "plied without labour, they will moſt certainly "remain idle; and to obtain this ſupply, they "are naturally tempted to fabricate falſehoods, "and impoſe themſelves as objects of charity on "the officer, or the magiſtrate. Indeed, when "their diſtreſſes are real, they are commonly "produced by that idleneſs and diſſipation, which "their dependance upon this parochial relief "encourages and promotes." As the diffuſion of the knowledge of the beſt means of remedying ſuch evils muſt be beneficial, and as the beſt means of providing employment for the poor, and dependant on pariſh charity, may be conſidered a branch of the queſtion before us, I ſhall inſert in a note, the meaſures which have been adopted in the Shrewſbury Houſe of Induſtry; they are conſonant to reaſon and humanity, have been proved efficacious by experience,

rience, and ſhould be attended to in the eſtabliſhment of all ſimilar inſtitutions *.

Although

* " —To provide a comfortable aſylum for the de-
" ſerving poor, whom age, diſeaſe, or infirmity, have
" diſabled from purſuing their various employments, a
" *Houſe of Induſtry*, under the direction of a *Board*,
" ſufficiently numerous to attend to the various de-
" partments, which will demand their care, and by a
" well-digeſted plan, and regulations maturely weighed,
" to introduce that *method, and order*, which will greatly
" lighten the burden of this attendance.—In this houſe,
" to provide employment for thoſe poor, who are able
" to work, but are either averſe to labour, or cannot
" otherwiſe procure it—thoſe who are thrown upon the
" pariſh by the mandate of the magiſtrate, thoſe chil-
" dren whom it is obliged to take care of—and thoſe
" alſo whom the parents, though induſtrious, are not
" able to maintain —By firmneſs and reſolution, tem-
" pered with gentleneſs and humanity, to introduce
" and eſtabliſh among the members of this family a
" habit of labour, of cleanlineſs, and of decency—To
" provide therein, for the regular daily diſcharge of
" thoſe religious duties, which have a tendency to cor-
" rect their morals—And moſt eſpecially to furniſh
" the means of inſtruction for children, and youth;
" and by a *total and complete ſeparation of theſe from the*
" *abandoned and depraved*, to place them out of the way
" of temptation, and prevent the fatal contagion of
" profligate diſcourſe, and vicious example—To encou-
" rage

Although it is to be concluded, however, that both ſupporting indolence, and rewarding with diſproportionate liberality, exertions of a ſlight, temporary, and deſultory nature, are incentives to idleneſs, and obſtacles to induſtry; yet it is not to be at the ſame time concluded, that the patient, perſevering, ſyſtematic labourer can in general be too amply rewarded. On the contrary, where the working claſs are of this deſcription, I am convinced, that "the liberal re-" ward of labour, as it encourages the propa-" gation, ſo it increaſes the induſtry, of the " common people." This maxim, however, muſt be received with ſome reſtrictions, which we ſhall endeavour to point out. We ſhall next endeavour to enforce the *general* juſtice of the obſervation,

" rage *all* by treating them with humanity, and good " humour, *diſtributing among them ſuitable rewards*, in " proportion to their induſtry, and good conduct; and " to puniſh the refractory, and diſorderly, by withhold-" ing thoſe rewards, by ſolitary confinement, or in ex-" treme caſes by corporal puniſhment." The particular bye-laws and regulations, by which theſe are effected, will be beſt underſtood by conſulting the pamphlet, intitled "*Some Account of the Shrewſbury Houſe of In-" duſtry*," &c. 1791. 8vo.

obſervation, and to anſwer the arguments adduced in oppoſition to it.

One exception to the univerſal application of this maxim, is that juſt now noticed, viz. that where the exertions of the labourer are ſlight, temporary, and deſultory, high rewards, in place of increaſing his induſtry, will always promote idleneſs and diſſipation. The maxim would alſo appear inapplicable to any people who worked merely for ſubſiſtence, and among whom no taſte for the artificial neceſſaries of life prevailed; and this would particularly be the caſe if they were addicted to idle amuſements, drunkenneſs, or any other ſpecies of debauchery. Among ſuch a people, any conſiderable increaſe in wages, or the other rewards of labour, unleſs very cautiouſly and gradually introduced, would be diſſipated in gratifying the vicious inclinations they are ſubject to; and in place of increaſing their induſtry, would produce the oppoſite baneful effect.

But however well-founded theſe, or any other partial exceptions may be, the general juſtice

of

of the poſition under conſideration cannot well be controverted. " The wages of labour," as Smith obſerves, " are the encouragement of in-" duſtry, which, like every other human qua-" lity, improves in proportion to the encou-" ragement it receives." It will accordingly, on examination, be diſcovered, that where the wages of labour are high, the labourer will be always found more induſtrious and laborious, than where they are low ; in England and Holland, for inſtance, than in Ireland or France. And we thence may deduce the reaſon, why manufactures will not fly to thoſe countries where the price of labour is low, though ſuch are the fears of every ſhort-ſighted and ſelfiſh individual engaged in them. On the contrary, we always find the wages of labour comparatively high, wherever manufactures are eſtabliſhed ; and wherever they are introduced, wages will always riſe. But we deviate from the ſubject before us. The circumſtance was introduced to ſhew, that high rewards and wages in general increaſe the induſtry of the people. They not only increaſe their induſtry, in the proper acceptation of the term, but they ſtimulate them to greater per-

ſonal

ſonal and bodily exertions. Of this we have daily inſtances in labourers ſet to work by *the piece.* We have alſo, among many others, a ſtriking proof of it in Mr. Young's Tour through Ireland. " Though my reſidence in Ireland," ſays he, " was not long enough to become a " perfect maſter of the queſtion, yet I have " employed from twenty to fifty men for ſe- " veral months, and found their habitual lazi- " neſs, or weakneſs, ſo great, whether work- " ing by meaſure, or by day, that I am abſo- " lutely convinced that one ſhilling and ſixpence, " or even two ſhillings a-day in Suffolk or Hert- " fordſhire, is much cheaper than ſixpence-half- " penny at Mitchelſtown——yet I have known " the Iriſh reapers in Hertfordſhire work as la- " boriouſly as any of our own men, and living " upon potatoes, which they procured from Lon- " don, but drinking nothing but ale."

The liberal reward of labour, beſides its immediate effect in increaſing the induſtry and exertions of the individual, has a ſimilar tendency indirectly, by the encouragement it gives to population. Where the wages of the labourer are

more

more than adequate to his immediate ſubſiſtence, the natural tendency which man in general feels to matrimonial connection, is not checked, by reflecting on the impoſſibility of ſupporting a family on thoſe earnings, which are barely adequate to the ſupply of one. Beſides, where the earnings of the parent are conſiderable, children are not only produced, but arrive at maturity: an event frequently, I fear, prevented by low wages, and conſequent poverty, wretched covering, and ſcanty and unwholeſome food. But to what more powerful incentive to induſtry, labour, and frugality can we have recourſe than the wants and claims of a numerous and riſing progeny? they ſtimulate the parent to every exertion, and copying his example, become in their turn induſtrious and uſeful members of ſociety.

In oppoſition to the opinion, that high wages encourage induſtry, it has been ſaid, that in dear years the working claſs are more induſtrious and inclined to labour, than in cheap ones; and as their wages are *nominally* the ſame in both caſes, they muſt *in effect* be higher in cheap than

in

in dear ſeaſons, and this variation is, therefore, a proof, that the liberal reward of labour does not produce the effect of increaſing the induſtry and application of the workman. To do away this concluſion, it may, in the firſt place, be remarked, that the obſervation is by no means univerſally juſt. Doctor Smith could not find, upon examination, that the variation of the produce of the linen manufacture in Scotland, or of the woollen manufacture in Yorkſhire, bore any ſenſible connection with the dearneſs or cheapneſs of the ſeaſons; and Monſieur Meſſance, a very reſpectable French author, ſhews, by comparing the produce of three extenſive manufactures in wool, linen, and ſilk, that the poor do *more* work in cheap than dear years. The obſervation has, indeed, been generally made by thoſe whoſe intereſt warped their ideas upon the ſubject; by maſters of every denomination, who generally find they can make better bargains with journeymen, and ſervants, in dear than in cheap years; which ariſes partly from the increaſed demand for them in cheap ſeaſons, partly from ſeveral journeymen working for themſelves in the ſame cheap years, which they

cannot

cannot accomplifh in dear ones. But this is no proof that the *general* induftry of the fociety is diminifhed by cheap feafons, or liberal wages *.

If liberal wages ever do difcourage induftry, it muft be the induftry of the wretch who works for mere fubfiftence, or the forced induftry of the indolent and diffolute; and even to produce this effect, the increafe muft be fudden and tranfitory, not gradual and permanent: a fettled liberal reward of labour can never produce fuch an effect. Of this, and of the general juftice of the pofition we wifh to eftablifh, there is a ftriking proof, the ufual effects of emigration to America on the labouring poor of European countries; the wages of all kinds of labour are there confiderably higher than thofe they have been accuftomed to receive; yet in place

* The people called *Drapers* in the North of Ireland, are all defirous to have provifions high; they never wifh to fee oat-meal under one penny per pound. They can in fuch cafes extort better bargains from the weavers. See Young. I am happy to fee our government, more enlightened, give a bounty on the importation of corn to the manufacturing counties, when above a certain price.

place of checking their induſtry, this in general produces a contrary effect. Their views become enlarged, they ſtore up the overplus of their wages till they can work for themſelves, or purchaſe a plantation and turn farmers: and thus, notwithſtanding the continual influx and increaſe of inhabitants, the demand for labour is conſtant, the labourer is liberally recompenſed, becomes induſtrious himſelf, and the means of exerting and rewarding induſtry in others.

Although the reward of labour ſhould be *nominally* high, yet from different cauſes the artificial neceſſaries of life may be ſo dear, that the overplus remaining, after providing actual ſubſiſtence, may be inadequate to the purchaſe of them. A taſte and deſire for ſuch neceſſaries, however, we have ſhewn to be one great ſource of individual and national induſtry. The government of a country ſhould, therefore, ſtudiouſly avoid raiſing the price of ſuch articles by taxation. To this circumſtance, however, ſufficient attention has not, I fear, been paid. The taxes on ſoap, leather, and the coarſer kind of manufactures deſtined for the conſumption of

the

the poor, which are levied in different countries, are all of the nature alluded to. Such taxes produce one immediately detrimental effect; that of raising the price of different manufactures, and thereby depriving a country of foreign trade, and lucrative export. This they effect, by necessarily raising the workman's wages; a rise which to him is only nominal, as he is as badly able as before such addition to purchase the different articles he has occasion for. But their effects are, perhaps, even more detrimental in the other way; especially in countries where a spirit of industry has not been established, but is to be excited and nourished. If the working class find it impossible by every exertion to obtain an overplus, after procuring actual subsistence, sufficient to enable them to purchase the artificial necessaries of life, they will entirely abandon such expectations; and, deprived of this spur to industry, labour, and exertion, will sink into indolence, content with the mere materials of wretched existence. Let the financier, then, reflect, that by levying a supply from the comforts and necessaries of the workman, he not only injures his country in the foreign market, but checks the induſtry of its natives, by depriving them of a principal incitement to labour; and renders their habitations the abodes of wretchedneſs, miſery, and indolence.

Such are the principal cautions to be obſerved, if we wiſh to render the imitative propenſity of man, and his deſire of enjoying the artificial neceſſaries of life, the means of making him induſtrious and laborious. Let us next conſider what other expedients may be had recourſe to with the greateſt proſpect of ſucceſs.

The man of fortune, which ariſes from an annual income or revenue, and who ſpends that revenue in ſupplying the various wants of himſelf and family, no doubt promotes induſtry, in ſo far as he is a purchaſer of the different articles of conſumption produced by different workmen and artiſts. A conſiderable part, however, of the revenue of ſuch an individual, is ſpent in the ſupport of menial ſervants, and attendants of different deſcriptions, whoſe labour is loſt to ſociety as not being realized in any article of manufacture or rude produce; and who, in in place of earning the wages of induſtry, may in general be ſaid to live upon the bread of idleneſs. The example of the family of ſuch a citizen, likewiſe, from which induſtry is uſually completely baniſhed, has neceſſarily the effect of diminiſhing the induſtry of its neighbours and dependents. The indirect encouragement to the induſtry of his country, which ſuch a citizen gives, will be ſtill diminiſhed, if a conſiderable part of his revenue is ſpent in articles produced by foreign labour.

On the other hand, the man of buſineſs, who, in place of living on revenue, employs a capital in any branch of agriculture or manufactures, ſets an example of induſtry, which is transfuſed among all connected with him, ſupports a multitude of hands, whoſe labour is realized, and whoſe wages are rated in proportion to their utility, application and induſtry.

The employment of *capital*, therefore, in any country, is a principal encouragement to the induſtry of its inhabitants. The celebrated Doctor Smith deems it its chief ſource and ſupport. " The proportion," ſays he, " between " capital and revenue ſeems every where to re- " gulate the proportion between induſtry and " idleneſs: every increaſe or diminution of ca- " pital, therefore, naturally tends to increaſe or " diminiſh the real quantity of induſtry, the " number of productive hands, and conſequently " the exchangeable value of the annual produce " of the land and labour of the country, the " real wealth and revenue of all its inhabi- " tants."

This may be deemed rather noticing a fact in the hiſtory of national induſtry, than developing the means of rendering a nation induſtrious. The accumulation of capital preſuppoſes ſome degree of induſtry; its application and employment are the effects of a continuation of the ſame principle. But in this, as in ſeveral other inſtances, effects become in their turn cauſes, more powerful in their operation than thoſe which originally produced them. Induſtry, like fame, acquires additional vigour in its progreſs, and every individual of her family becomes in turn the

the parent of an offspring, equally prolific and beneficial as the original ſtock.

Beſides the influence already noticed, by which the imitative propenſity of man becomes the means of rendering him induſtrious; when induſtry is once ſet on ſoot, the power of example, as above hinted, tends in another manner to extend and increaſe it. "The human mind," ſays Hume, "is of a very imitative nature, nor "is it poſſible for any ſet of men to converſe "often together, without acquiring a ſimilitude "of manners, and communicating to each other "their vices as well as virtues. The propenſity "to company and ſociety, is ſtrong in all ra- "tional creatures; and the ſame diſpoſition which "gives us this propenſity, makes us enter deep- "ly into each other's ſentiments, and cauſes like "paſſions and inclinations to run, as it were "by contagion, through the whole club or knot "of companions. Where a number of men are "united into one political body, the occaſions of "their intercourſe muſt be ſo frequent, for de- "fence, commerce, or government, that, toge- "ther with the ſame ſpeech and language, they

" muſt acquire a reſemblance in their manners; " and have a common or national character, as " well as a perſonal one, peculiar to each indi- " vidual."

On this principle, there certainly is a foundation for the opinion, that every nation is marked by ſome peculiar character; and with reſpect to induſtrious purſuits, we have a ſtriking inſtance of its effects in Holland, where it is unfaſhionable for a man not to be employed in ſome ſpecies of buſineſs; and whenever, in any country, a number of its inhabitants come to be employed in induſtrious occupations, their example alone, independent of the intrinſic attractions of induſtry, will lead others into ſimilar purſuits.

Although the legiſlature of a country cannot force its ſubjects to induſtry and labour, it may give them indirect encouragement thereto, by checking ſuch practices as are moſt detrimental to its progreſs. Of ſuch practices none are more injurious, to none are a poor and indolent people more inclined, than drunkenneſs; nor is there any,

any, perhaps, not liable to immediate puniſhment, which can be more effectually checked by the proper exertions of legiſlative power. To this purpoſe ſtatutes will avail but little; the plain and efficacious mode appears to be, taxing the materials of ebriety, whether directly or indirectly, ſo high, as to render the gratification of the deſire extremely difficult to the lower and laborious claſs. If a beverage can be diſcovered, poſſeſſed of the exhilarating powers of ſpirituous liquors, properly ſo called, but not liable to the ſame abuſe, and at the ſame time ſtrengthening and nutritious, that ſhould certainly be afforded them at the cheapeſt rate poſſible. Such we well know to be thoſe generally termed Malt Liquors; on theſe, the taxes, if *any* be levied, ſhould be as light as poſſible: on thoſe of a contrary deſcription, they ſhould be proportionately heavy. Let not the circumſtance of a ſlight alteration in the amount of the revenue, influence, in this inſtance, the determinations of the legiſlator. If any deficiency is occaſioned by the meaſure, let it rather be made up in ſome other mode. The ſtateſman is to look forward to conſequences; his views ſhould be enlarged; and

if

if he extends them, he muſt perceive, that the prevalence of drunkenneſs will in the end injure the revenue of a ſtate, infinitely more than any temporary loſs, which can be otherwiſe ſupplied. Need the effects of that vice be particularly detailed, which ruins the health of the labourer, checks the population of a country, diſſipates the funds, and annihilates the ſpirit of induſtry, and ſpreads its baneful contagion from an individual through his ſtarving family, from ſtarving families through an idle and impoveriſhed nation? No; its effects are too viſible, wherever its prevalence is experienced; and too injurious not to require every exertion and ſacrifice towards its extirpation.

The legiſlature of a country may alſo excite and ſupport a ſpirit of induſtry among the people, by providing a proper and univerſal ſyſtem of education. It is equally extraordinary, and to be regretted, that in all governments, any plan of education which might embrace the children of the inferior orders ſeems to have been neglected. Education, however, is the power which principally forms the character of an individual; and were a plan

plan of the nature alluded to devifed, and properly conducted, to no principle of greater efficacy could we poffibly have recourfe, towards reforming or modelling the manners of a people. As a differtation on this fubject, however, has already been honoured by the Academy with a prize, any further remarks may here be deemed fuperfluous. The fubject does honour to their choice, and it is to be hoped our nation will foon fee fome fuch fyftem carried into execution.

The legiflature may alfo promote the induftry of a nation, by encouraging particular branches of employment. But of this we muft naturally defer the difcuffion to the third fection. At prefent, let it fuffice to obferve, that however upright and benevolent the intention may be, meafures of this nature fhould be adopted with the greateft caution. The moft difcerning politician is at beft but fhort-fighted: particular branches of induftry may be encouraged, nay, principally fupported, at the expence, and to the depreffion of others, more beneficial to the ftate, and more productive of employment to the community.

munity. The ſelfiſh views of individuals, combine with the natural intricacy of the general intereſts of a nation, to deceive and miſlead the ſtateſman, and to render ſuch attempts the moſt delicate and difficult he can poſſibly undertake.

Such appear to be the principal general meaſures, which can be directly employed, towards exciting a ſpirit of induſtry among the people; and from a review of them it will be evident—that its progreſs muſt at firſt be naturally ſlow—that the immediate means which can be employed by any legiſlature towards its encouragement and diſſemination, are neceſſarily tedious and feeble in their operation—and that it is from the operation of that natural tendency and deſire, which almoſt every man feels of bettering his ſituation, we are chiefly to expect its commencement, propagation, and increaſe.

Though the legiſlature of a ſtate, however, be naturally cramped and confined, in the direct means which can be recurred to for rendering a people induſtrious, they can indirectly facilitate

tate and promote its progreſs, to a very conſiderable degree, by removing or diminiſhing thoſe impediments to its free exertion, which the enlightened politician will find exiſting, in greater or leſs proportion, in almoſt every ſtate. This naturally leads to the ſecond ſection of our ſubject, which we ſhall next proceed to conſider.

SECTION II.

On the principal Impediments to Induſtry and Labour which exiſt under different Forms of Government.

Difficulty of removing the impediments to induſtry —Want of general liberty—Proofs of its impeding and depreſſing induſtry—From a review of the hiſtory of induſtrious nations—From the hiſtory of the riſe of induſtry in the middle ages—From tracing the progreſs of induſtry—Inſecurity of property—Inſtances of this—Injudicious taxes—General errors in taxation—Taxes on neceſſaries —Taxes raiſed from, and proportioned to the produce of induſtry—Tithe—Perſonal taille—Taxes on the wages of labour—Taxes impeding the operations of induſtry—Internal duties—Alcavala —Taxes on materials employed in induſtry—Taxes on exportation—Corporations—impede induſtry and employment in two ways—by forming excluſive companies; and, levying taxes and tolls—Excluſive companies.

SECTION II.

THE removal of every impediment or obſtruction to induſtry and labour, and conſequently to the employment of the people, forms a neceſſary and intereſting diviſion of the ſubject before us. The writer, however, who attempts to enumerate ſuch impediments, to develope their injurious tendency, and to enforce by argument the neceſſity of their correction or removal, aſſumes, as far as ſpeculation goes, the functions of a ſtate reformer; a character, in general, diſliked at once, and uſeleſs: diſliked, becauſe interfering with the intereſts of many; uſeleſs, becauſe neglected, or ſucceſsfully counteracted and oppoſed.

It is impoſſible to diſcover any error in the politics and conſtitution of a ſtate, in the continuation of which, many individuals are not perſonally intereſted. Such will always with clamour and outcry oppoſe any innovation, however conſiderable the benefits to ſociety at large, by which it may be attended; ſuch will ever depreciate the views, arraign the motives, and counteract the exertions, of the perſon who may propoſe the alteration. It is to be lamented that in general the efforts of theſe characters have been too ſucceſsful; and that where the injurious nature of many inſtitutions is as certain, as that their correction or removal would be beneficial, the oppoſition to ſuch change has been frequently crowned with ſucceſs, and has perpetuated, or at leaſt prolonged, their exiſtence.

But however ſlight may be our expectations of introducing the changes, or effecting the improvement, here alluded to; it is the duty of the Eſſayiſt upon the preſent ſubject, to expoſe thoſe cauſes which may impede or prevent the employment of the people; and conſequently to notice the errors and vices in government and politics which produce ſuch effects.

Deferring to the ſecond part, any circumſtances of this nature, which particularly affect the Iriſh nation, we ſhall here confine ourſelves to thoſe

moſt

moſt univerſally exiſting, and moſt general in their operation.

The firſt circumſtance I ſhall notice, as counteracting the ſpirit of induſtry, and conſequently obſtructing or preventing the employment of a people, is, *the want of general liberty.* This is an obſtruction to employment, which in our iſlands is happily unknown. It has, however, exiſted there—it ſtill exiſts in ſeveral nations, and its pernicious operation is as conſtant, as conſiderable. To define the preciſe nature and extent of liberty, neceſſary to the ſupport and advancement of induſtry, would be extremely difficult, and is a taſk I ſhall not attempt. From general conſideration it would appear, that that ſtate enjoys a degree of liberty ſufficient to the encouragement of induſtry, wherein, 1. The laws are not liable to be changed at the arbitrary will of any individual, and are enacted by an aſſembly elected from the people. 2. Where every individual enjoys equal protection and ſecurity from the laws; and, 3. Where taxes are aſſeſſed by a ſimilar aſſembly, and levied indiſcriminately on all ranks.

Minutely

Minutely to develope the particular modes, by which the want of general liberty repreſſes the induſtry, and checks the employment of a people, would ſeem a tedious, and in a great degree an unneceſſary taſk. Many of the impediments which we ſhall ſhortly notice, are the progeny of deſpotiſm, and an explanation of their injurious tendency, will in a great meaſure unfold the principal cauſes immediately deſtructive of induſtry, reſulting from ſuch a form of government. It here ſeems ſufficient to prove in general, that the want of liberty is a conſiderable bar and impediment to the induſtrious exertions of man; and this proof we ſhall deduce, from a wide and rapid ſurvey, of the hiſtory, and preſent ſituation, of different nations.

If we conſider the different appearance of thoſe countries, which once poſſeſſed a free form of government, but which at preſent labour under the oppreſſion of deſpotiſm, we ſhall find that ſuch a change has almoſt uniformly produced the effect of annihilating their induſtry, manufactures, and commerce. Tyre, at firſt poſſeſſed of freedom, was the parent of that trade and induſtry, which has ſince enriched ſo many nations. Greece, enjoying a ſtill greater degree of liberty, was rouſed by her example, became, as well as her free colonies on the coaſt of Aſia, the principal ſeat of the commerce and induſtry of the world, and continued ſuch while their freedom laſted. Carthage, the child of Tyre, ſurpaſſed even her parent, as well in liberty as in trade; poſſeſſed both of the richeſt regions of Africa, and the fertile provinces of Spain, her fleets covered all the then navigated parts of the ocean, and her commerce and induſtry, population and riches, increaſed, till ruined by the conqueſt and deſpotiſm of Rome. All theſe countries, however, ſo bleſt in ſituation, fertility, and natural productions, exhibit at preſent the moſt inſtructive inſtances of the effects of deſpotic power. Reduced and degraded by its oppreſſion, their population has been diminiſhed, commerce, except that of ſtrangers, baniſhed from their ſhores, and the ſpirit of induſtry and labour completely annihilated.

The impediments and obſtructions to trade and induſtry, which neceſſarily reſult from a deſ-

potic

potic and ſlaviſh form of government, and the encouragement they receive from the enjoyment of a competent degree of liberty, are ſtrikingly exemplified in the hiſtory of the revival of trade, commerce, and manufactures, in Europe. The ſpirit of the feodal form of government, which ſo univerſally prevailed in all European ſtates, was ſuch, that while it allowed almoſt unreſtrained licenſe to a few powerful barons, it ſubjected the great body of the people to the oppreſſion of arbitrary and unlimited authority. Induſtry and the arts were accordingly almoſt completely extirpated, commerce was nearly unknown, and the few and miſerable itinerant traders who continued its ſemblance, were expoſed to exactions and inſults the moſt diſcouraging and oppreſſive. Venice, ſheltered by her ſituation from the oppreſſion and deſpotiſm to which other ſtates were expoſed, acquired a degree of liberty in her government which gave birth to, and cheriſhed induſtry, manufactures, and commerce. Genoa and Piſa, acquiring a ſimilar degree of freedom, became her rivals in trade; their liberty and induſtry were in the ſame degree progreſſive, and received reciprocal

aſſiſtance

aſſiſtance from each other. Remote from the reſidence of their German ſovereigns, many other cities of Italy made ſimilar ſucceſſive efforts, and acquired that liberty and independence, which, wherever eſtabliſhed, proved ſtrikingly beneficial.

Actuated by motives of ſelf-intereſt, rather than enlarged and liberal views of policy, the other ſovereigns of the middle ages, deſirous of curbing the power of the barons, conferred particular privileges on cities, ſimilar to thoſe the Italian ſtates had acquired by their own exertions, and thus exempted their inhabitants from the oppreſſion to which the other ſubjects of the ſtate were expoſed. "This acquiſition of liber-"ty," as the hiſtorian of Charles the Fifth obſerves, "made ſuch a happy change in the con-"dition of all the members of ſuch communi-"ties, as rouſed them from that ſtupidity and "inaction, into which they had been ſunk by "the wretchedneſs of their former ſtate. The "ſpirit of induſtry revived, commerce became "an object of attention, and began to flouriſh; "population increaſed; independence was eſta-

 "bliſhed;

" bliſhed; and wealth flowed into cities, which " had long been the ſeat of poverty and op- " preſſion." Poland, even at preſent, affords us a memorable inſtance of the deſtructive tendency of that form of government, wherein the *few* were lawleſs maſters, the *multitude* miſerable ſlaves. The feodal ſyſtem has continued with little melioration or change: the country which it oppreſſes, notwithſtanding the general improvement of Europe, remains beggarly, diſtreſſed, and miſerable; and its inhabitants ſhould ever execrate the deſpot, who has too ſucceſsfully oppoſed a revolution, which every liberal mind muſt wiſh is only deferred to a more favourable opportunity.

If we perſiſt in tracing the progreſs of induſtry and trade, after their firſt revival, the general poſition intended to be eſtabliſhed will be further confirmed; and we ſhall find, that liberty is as neceſſary to their increaſe and continuance, as to their birth and origin. This appears abundantly evident from the hiſtory of thoſe ſtates, which have moſt excelled in commerce and induſtry: they have been almoſt uniformly

formly bleſſed with liberty, and a free form of government. Of ſuch we have only to cite from antiquity, the inſtances of Athens, Rhodes, the Grecian colonies in Aſia, and Carthage; from the middle ages, Venice, Genoa, and the cities of the Hanſeatick league; and in modern days we are furniſhed with ſimilar proofs, by England, Holland, and the free ſtates of America.

The next obſtacle to the induſtry and employment of a people we ſhall notice, and which, indeed, is generally experienced in deſpotic governments only, is

Inſecurity of property. Wherever the acquiſitions of labour, induſtry, and frugality, are not held ſacred, and protected from the graſp of power, their exertions will be more effectually repreſſed, than by any other expedient whatever. The rapine and exactions of the baſhaws of Turkey, are alone ſufficient to keep its trade and induſtry in a ſtate of perpetual infancy: even in the more moderate governments of Spain, and France before the late revolution, contributions ſimilar in their nature, though levied with more formality, and lefs violence, have had their fhare in depreffing the commerce and induftry of thofe nations. But deferring to the head of *improper taxes*, the confideration of thofe impediments, I fhall here only notice a few of the exactions which in the middle ages fubfifted in every country in Europe, and which are ftill obfervable in many.

Independent of the occafional and arbitrary demands, frequently made by rapacious princes and barons on their inferiors, they often raifed contributions for real or imaginary fervices. Such were the recompences given for the protection of a powerful lord; the fine of a year's rent paid on the inveftiture of an eftate; the payment of a minor's income during his minority to his fuperiors, referving only the fum adequate to his immediate fupport. Of a fimilar nature were the prefents made on the wedding of the baron's eldeft fon. The mockery of juftice was alfo rendered the means of extracting contributions: the fifth part of the value of every fubject, the property of which was tried in his court, was paid to the baron. The inftitution of *purveyance*, which

which ſtill ſubſiſts in every monarchy in Europe, (England, and France ſince the revolution, excepted) is another inſtance of oppreſſive exaction, and inſecurity of property. When the king's troops, or his attendants, or officers of any deſcription, paſſed through the country, the peaſants were obliged to furniſh them with carriages, horſes, proviſions, and other conveniencies, at a price which an attendant officer, termed a *purveyor*, regulated at diſcretion. When a peaſant took any portion of land by leaſe, he was liable, beſide paying the rent, and performing the other covenants it contained, to certain ſervices not ſtipulated therein, and which being ſuppoſed to be regulated by the cuſtom of the barony, were in a great meaſure arbitrary, and frequently infringed on the property of the tenant. It is not long ſince this cuſtom was aboliſhed in Scotland.—But it is needleſs to perſiſt in ſtating the various modes of exaction, purſued in the days of barbariſm, or which are ſtill obſervable in deſpotic governments. It is equally needleſs to adduce any arguments to prove, that all ſimilar inſtitutions, in ſo far as they render property inſecure, are detrimental to induſtry. Why ſhould man labour for the acquiſition of a prize, a prize, the poſſeſſion of which is uncertain, and dependent on the will of *one* or *many* tyrants?

A conſiderable number of the impediments to induſtry, and conſequent obſtruction to the employment of the people, may be ranked under the head of,

Injudicious taxes. Theſe we ſhall accordingly proceed to conſider particularly, premiſing a few obſervations on injudicious taxation in general. A tax is that portion of his revenue, which every individual pays towards the ſupport of the government under which he lives, and by which his property, from whatever ſource it ariſes, is protected. It is the reſignation of part of his wealth, for the protection and preſervation of the remainder. The contribution ſhould, therefore, be as juſtly as poſſible proportioned to the value of the poſſeſſion, towards the preſervation of which it is contributed. Such proportionate aſſeſſment we ſhall call the *equality of taxation*, every deviation from it a degree of *inequality*, which, as principally oppreſſive to the lower and laborious

laborious order of the people, muſt ever prove impolitic, injurious, and deſtructive of induſtry. The amount of the contribution granted for the purpoſes above ſtated ſhould ever be clearly defined, and aſcertained, and not ſubject in the moſt remote degree to the determination or caprice of the aſſeſſor or collector. Any deviation from this maxim occaſions an *incertainty* in taxation, as oppreſſive to the inferior part of the community, and conſequently as injurious to their induſtry and employment, as the *inequality* juſt noticed.

Theſe appear to be the two leading and univerſally injurious errors to be avoided in the impoſition of taxes. They have not, however, been always avoided ; and, as inſtances, we ſhall, out of many others, adduce an example of each, which exiſted in France before the late revolution. The nobility and clergy, who poſſeſſed the greateſt portion of revenue, and who conſequently ſhould in the ſame proportion contribute more than any others to the exigencies of the ſtate, were totally exempt from the land-tax, which conſequently fell on the induſtrious labourer.

bourer. This was an inequality indefenfible on any rational principles, degrading in its *appcarance*, ruinous in its effects. An example of deftructive *incertainty* of taxation could have been furnifhed by the fame unfortunate country. In the collection of what was called the *perfonal taille*, every contributor was affeffed in proportion to what was fuppofed his ability of payment; but this ability was determined at will, by certain parifh officers, whom ignorance, malice, animofity, or refentment might, and undoubtedly did, upon feveral occafions, miflead. No man could be certain of the amount of his contribution. His property was in a great degree at the mercy of petty and interefted defpots, and his induftry was confequently checked, oppreffed, or annihilated. Thefe two defects in taxation, Inequality and Incertainty, are the *generally* operating errors deftructive of induftry, to be carefully avoided or meliorated. Let us next confider more particularly what are the *fpecies* of taxation which principally injure and reprefs the induftry and employment of a people. Thefe may be arranged under three heads; the firft, comprehending taxes which increafe the price of

the

the neceſſaries of life. The ſecond, taxes raiſed from, and proportioned to, the produce of induſtry. And the third, including thoſe which impede the operations of induſtry.

1. Any taxes, levied on the *artificial* neceſſaries of life, muſt inevitably raiſe their price, and render their acquiſition more difficult to the inferior and labouring orders of the people; but the ſpirit of induſtry, as has already been ſhewn, ariſes in a great degree from the deſire of acquiring theſe neceſſaries, and will, therefore, be checked by any aſſeſſment which raiſes their price ſo high as to place them beyond the reach of theſe claſſes of the community. The operation of ſuch taxes, in this way, has been already explained. Taxes on the *abſolute* neceſſaries of life are equally deſtructive, and where both are conjoined, the diſcouragement to employment they occaſion muſt be equally certain and conſiderable. If by ſuch taxes the price of the neceſſaries of life is raiſed ſo high, as that the earnings of induſtrious labour are not equal to their purchaſe, he who is rouſed to daily exertions by the preſſing calls of nature, finding

all

all his efforts inadequate to their gratification, will either expire in misery, support a useless, indolent and miserable existence on the scanty supplies of charity, or, spurred on to desperation, will brave the laws and disturb the order of society, and in rapine seek that relief which the steadiest exertions of industry could not furnish.

Hear the opinion of the eloquent Raynal on the effects of such injudicious imposts. "Mais
" si la taxe porte sur les denrées de premier be-
" soin, c'est le comble de la cruauté. Avant
" toutes les loix sociales, l'homme avoit le
" droit de subsister: l'a-t-il perdu par l'établisse-
" ment des loix? Survendre aux peuple les fruits
" de la terre, c'est lui ravir par un impot, les
" moyens naturel de la conserver. En pressu-
" rant la subsistance de l'indigent, l'état lui
" ote les forces, avec les alimens. D'un homme
" pauvre, il fait un mendiant, d'un travailleur,
" un oisif; d'un malheureux, un scélérat; c'est
" à dire qu'il conduit un famélique à l'echa-
" faud par la misere."

Befide their immediate effects on the individual, fuch taxes are deftructive to the induftry and employment of a people in two other ways, by checking population, and raifing the price of manufactured produce deftined for exportation.

The more populous any country is, the more confiderable will be the demand for the different articles, abfolutely, or artificially, neceffary to life; the raifing and manufacturing fuch are the principal fources of employment; but how can be devifed a more effectual bar to population, than fcanty or difficultly acquired fubfiftence, which prevents matrimonial connection, or, if fuch connection takes place, renders its progeny feeble, or prematurely deprives them of exiftence.

Taxes on the natural or artificial neceffaries of life, muft raife, in a greater or lefs degree, the wages of labour. Any increafe in the wages of labour muft neceffarily raife the price of thofe articles, in the produce or manufacture of which it is employed; and this rife, if confiderable, will inevitably deprive any country of the foreign

market

market for ſuch commodities, and diſcourage their conſumption in the home. Nay, in time, prohibitory laws will not prevent foreigners from ſupplying even the home market with ſuch articles: when the temptation becomes conſiderable enough, they will be introduced by ſmuggling, and their manufacture or cultivation be completely annihilated. Theſe obſervations hold particularly as to manufactures, and where, as in the modern ſtates of Europe, the employment of ſo many hands depends upon their flouriſhing condition, the ſtateſman cannot be too cautious of adopting any meaſure which may tend to depreſs or deſtroy them. The deſtructive tendency of taxes on the neceſſaries of life has been long experienced in Holland; and the injuries they occaſion are daily increaſing. Almoſt every neceſſary of life is there highly taxed; even flour, when ground at the mill, or baked at the oven, pays a duty. Similar impoſitions take place in Genoa, Modena, and many other Italian ſtates. De Wit obſerves, that in his time ſuch multiplied taxes had raiſed the price of Dutch cloth forty per cent.; and they have at length almoſt entirely deſtroyed their once flouriſhing manufactures in wool, ſilk, gold, ſilver, and other materials. The general decay of their trade is probably to be attributed, in a great meaſure, to the ſame cauſe; and if England be not cautious, ſhe may in time experience the ſame misfortune.

2. The next diviſion we ſhall conſider is that of taxes raiſed from, and proportioned to, the produce of induſtry. Were a man of ſound, common ſenſe, and general obſervation, requeſted to deviſe the moſt effectual and practicable expedient, next to that of abſolute prohibition, for impeding the exertions of induſtry, he would, it is moſt likely, propoſe a tax of the nature we have mentioned. If the legiſlature were deſirous of diſcouraging the proſecution of any particular manufacture, how could their intentions be more effectually anſwered, than by loading its produce with a certain impoſt, and proportioning its amount to that of the article manufactured? Such a tax would be neceſſarily injurious, in proportion to the value of the branch of induſtry affected by it particularly, and to the number of labourers employed in its proſecution.

Of

Of the various occupations in which mankind are employed, none, as we ſhall hereafter have occaſion to ſhew, are of ſuch importance, none afford employment to ſo many labourers, as agriculture. A tax, therefore, on its proſecution, of the nature we have deſcribed, muſt neceſſarily be an impoſition, injurious in its effects, general in its operation, and more efficacious than any other aſſeſſment, in diminiſhing the demand for labour, and checking the employment of the people; preciſely, however, of this nature is the tax termed

Tithe, which muſt always operate as a clog to induſtry, and an impediment to agricultural improvement; and this will be particularly the caſe, where it is rigorouſly exacted in kind, unleſs purchaſed at the full market price. The eſtabliſhment of what has been termed a *modus*, or a certain ſtated acreable compenſation, for the tithe of the different titheable articles of rude produce, would tend in a great degree to obviate the injurious effects of the tithe ſyſtem, as at preſent generally eſtabliſhed. The conſideration, that the church, which runs no riſk, and

lays

lays out no capital, is to derive an advantage from the moſt expenſive cultivation and improvement, proportionate to the induſtry, ſkill, attention and expence of the farmer, muſt undoubtedly check and conſiderably diſcourage his exertions. Were the amount of the tax *certain*, and not thus proportioned, the evil would be conſiderably meliorated.

The cultivation of madder, while the tithe of it was exacted in kind in England, was confined to Holland, where no ſuch tax is known; and the Engliſh dyers were obliged to reſort thither for the neceſſary ſupplies of this uſeful plant. A ſtatute was at length paſſed, enacting, that five ſhillings an acre ſhould be received, as a modus for all tithe of madder, and ſince that period its cultivation has been introduced, and is rapidly increaſing. The modus in lieu of the tithe of the rudiments of manufactures ſhould be light: in England that for flax and hemp is never to exceed five ſhillings per acre. As an encouragement to the reclaiming barren grounds, it would ſeem but reaſonable to exempt them from tithe for a certain period after their firſt cultivation:

the produce of ſuch lands is for ſome time, in general, little more than ſufficient to replace the capital laid out in their improvement. One would imagine the intereſts of the church ſhould lead them to concede to this indulgence, from which a conſiderable increaſe to their revenue muſt ultimately ariſe: in England, cultivated lands of this deſcription are tithe-free for ſeven years.'

Tithe, when rigorouſly exacted in kind, is conſiderably deſtructive in its effects, and particularly impedes the employment of the people, in thoſe countries where agriculture is in its infancy, and where little capital is poſſeſſed by the cultivators of the earth: this, however, we ſhall have a better opportunity of ſhewing when we come to treat of the particular circumſtances of Ireland; till which time we ſhall defer any further obſervations reſpecting it: ſuffice it here to remark, that, in ſuch countries, particular attention ſhould be paid to ſoften its rigours, and remedy its inconveniencies as much as poſſible.

The tax levied in France before the late revolution, under the name of the *perſonal taille*, is another inſtance of a deſtructive impoſt, proportioned to the ſuppoſed profits, and conſequently to the induſtry of the people. The injurious tendency of this tax, as an arbitrary and unequal one, we have already had occaſion to notice. Its having been proportioned to the profits of the farmer, rendered it doubly deſtructive and oppreſſive. The profits of the farmer were generally eſtimated by the ſtate of cultivation of the farm, and the quantity of ſtock he poſſeſſed upon it. To render the tax, therefore, light, he employed as little ſtock as poſſible, and the cultivation of his lands was proportionably wretched and miſerable: to increaſe his ſtock, to improve his cultivation, were certain means of augmenting his proportion of the aſſeſſment. If any capital accumulated in his hands, this was a certain prohibition againſt his laying it out on the farm; and it was equally efficacious in preventing thoſe already poſſeſſed of capital from employing it in agricultural improvement: a more abſurd and ruinous engine of extortion and oppreſſion, than an aſſeſſment of this nature, can

 ſcarcely

ſcarcely be deviſed. Almoſt equally injurious are *taxes on the wages of labour* ; the effects of which, as Smith juſtly obſerves, muſt be " the declen- " ſion of induſtry, the decreaſe of employment " for the poor, and the diminution of the an- " nual produce of the land and labour of the " country." Such taxes, however, have been, and are exacted. In France, before the revolution, the induſtry of day-labourers was rendered one of the ſources of revenue; their labour was eſtimated at two hundred working days in the year, from the ſcanty wages of which, a certain portion was ſubtracted, the amount of which varied from ſeaſon to ſeaſon, according to the judgment or caprice of the collector. In Bohemia artificers are divided into four claſſes; the firſt pay each to the amount of about nine pounds ſeven ſhillings and ſixpence a-year ; the ſecond, about ſix pounds eleven ſhillings and three-pence ; the third four pounds thirteen ſhillings and nine-pence ; and the fourth, half the latter ſum. *Capitation taxes*, when levied on the lower orders of the people, are to be conſidered in the ſame light as taxes on the wages of labour. Such claſſes in general poſſeſs no other ſource of payment.

3. A

3. A third diviſion of injurious taxes remains to be conſidered, including thoſe particularly affecting the operations of induſtry. Of theſe we ſhall notice ſome of the moſt remarkable. Every ſpecies of taxation, which interrupts or harraſſes the freedom of the internal trade of any country, is certainly a conſiderable impediment to the operations of induſtry: the interior commerce of any great nation, being that of the moſt conſiderable importance to its inhabitants; and the home market being neceſſarily the moſt extenſive and regular, for the different productions of their labour, both ſhould be as free as poſſible from duties, examination, or reſtriction. It is to the freedom of internal commerce which prevails in Great Britain, that Doctor Smith attributes in a great degree its riches and proſperity. Other countries, however, have not been ſo fortunate.

Nothing ſo effectually impedes the interior commerce of a country as its being laden with duties; eſpecially if they be not uniform. In France, previous to the late change of government, a different ſyſtem of taxation prevailed in different diſtricts; few goods could enter one province, or paſs through it to another, without paying certain impoſts, which varied in each, and for the collection of which their ſeveral frontiers were crowded and guarded by petty revenue officers. Even the neceſſary articles of life, as corn, wine, butchers meat, &c. paid different duties on paſſing the boundaries of provinces, or entering their great cities: theſe were called *péages*, or tranſit duties. The dutchies of Milan and Parma are in like manner divided into ſmall diſtricts, in all of which the different productions of the country are taxed, and in each upon a different ſyſtem.

Nothing can more effectually obſtruct the operations of induſtry, than taxes upon the ſale of different merchandizes: of this we have a notable example in the tax called *Alcavala* in Spain. This is a tax upon the ſale of every ſpecies of commodities. It was originally ten per cent. was raiſed by Philip III. and IV. to fourteen per cent. and at preſent is ſix per cent. *ad valorem*, repeated every time the article is ſold. Its collection neceſſarily requires a crowd

of

of revenue officers, who attend the goods from province to province, town to town, nay, ſhop to ſhop. Its effects, as may well be ſuppoſed, have been ruinous in the extreme: the declenſion of the Spaniſh commerce, manufactures, and induſtry, is well known; and Uſtaritz, their moſt ſenſible writer on theſe ſubjects, deems this tax the chief cauſe of their ruin.

Taxes on the different materials employed in the operations of induſtry are neceſſarily impediments of conſiderable efficacy. The tax of three ſhillings and three-pence per ton, levied in England on coal carried coaſtwiſe, deſerves to be ranked among the injurious taxes of this nature. Fuel is an article of abſolute neceſſity in almoſt all manufactures; we accordingly find them in England flouriſhing, in general, in coal counties, and languiſhing where this neceſſary article is deficient and dear. To levy a tax on its carriage to ſuch diſtricts is, therefore, an abſurd aſſeſſment, which increaſes the natural diſadvantages they labour under, and which repreſſes the induſtry, and obſtructs the employment of their inhabitants.

All

All taxes levied on the materials of manufactures will unavoidably check and obſtruct them: few examples, indeed, of this nature are obſervable. In ſome inſtances, even in England, where the nature of commerce is ſuppoſed to be beſt underſtood, taxes are impoſed on the importation of the *primum* of ſome manufactures, with a view of encouraging their production at home, and ſerving the landed intereſt: their good effects, however, in this way, would appear doubtful; their injurious tendency in the other, certain.

But if levying taxes on the importation of the primum of manufactures be, in general, at beſt a doubtful, and probably an injurious piece of policy; how much more deſtructive muſt be the loading with duties the produce or the manufactures of a country when exported?

In former ages, when the principles of commerce were little underſtood, heavy duties on exportation, or its abſolute prohibition, were deemed the moſt efficacious means of ſecuring plenty at home: thus, in Scotland, not only the different

different articles of rude produce, but various articles of manufactures, as linen, candles, hides, ſhoes, &c. were prohibited from being exported. At preſent, however, the general policy of European nations is diametrically oppoſite; and the cuſtomary practice is, to load with duties the importation of different manufactured articles from foreign ſtates, and to permit the exportation of ſuch from home duty free. Some writers have queſtioned the juſtice and policy of loading with heavy duties, or abſolutely prohibiting, the importation of foreign manufactures: their opinions on this point we ſhall hereafter have an opportunity of conſidering; but whatever doubts may be entertained reſpecting the impropriety of taxing importation, it will be univerſally agreed, that taxing or prohibiting the exportation, eſpecially of manufactures, muſt check the commerce, curb the induſtry, and obſtruct the employment of a people.

The next ſource of obſtruction and impediment to induſtry and employment which we ſhall notice, is the conferring particular privileges and immunities, on certain deſcriptions of the people.

The

The two principal inſtances of this nature which occur, and the only ones we ſhall conſider, are Corporations, and Trading Companies. And, firſt, of

Corporations. Induſtry, as has been already remarked, firſt reared its head during the rude and barbarous diſſipation and idleneſs of the middle ages, in enfranchiſed cities. The particular privileges conferred upon, or aſſumed by them, of enacting laws and regulations for their own government, was the immediate ſource of this improvement; inaſmuch as they were thereby enabled to protect and defend the liberties and property of their inhabitants. Actuated, however, by the ſpirit of monopoly, and, as may be well ſuppoſed, conſulting more their own immediate intereſt, than thoſe of ſociety at large, their ſubſequent regulations have uſually tended to impede the *general* induſtry and employment of the people. As the neceſſity for ſuch inſtitutions no longer exiſts, if any injuries reſult from their continuance, they certainly ſhould be aboliſhed, or their injurious tendency at leaſt corrected. They foſtered induſtry, no doubt, after its birth; but if the nurſes of infancy become

come a nuiſance to the adult, let them be curbed or diſcarded. Corporations ſeem to impede the induſtry and employment of a people principally in two ways; firſt, by forming excluſive companies, the freedom of which is neceſſary to the exerciſing its particular trade; and, ſecondly, by exacting taxes, tolls and impoſitions for the ſupport of a uſeleſs and indolent magiſtracy.

The freedom of the working companies of different corporations is generally obtained by ſerving an apprenticeſhip of a certain number of years to ſome individual of the company. Thoſe who have not ſerved ſuch apprenticeſhip are by the laws of the corporation prevented from exerciſing any trade within its juriſdiction. The effects of ſuch prohibition neceſſarily are, not only by diminiſhing the number of, and conſequently the competition among the workmen, to raiſe the price upon the conſumer, but to prevent any individuals, who may be otherwiſe perfectly well qualified, from procuring employment and ſubſiſtence for themſelves, or affording employment and ſubſiſtence to others. To diminiſh as much as poſſible the number of work-

men,

men, and conſequently the competition among them, corporate companies have not been always ſatisfied with enforcing a long apprenticeſhip, they ſometimes limit and regulate the number of apprentices which a maſter is to take. In Sheffield a cutler can have but one apprentice at a time, and in Norfolk no weaver can have more than two. Nay, in Germany, there frequently is a determined number of tradeſmen allowed to every corporation, which cannot be exceeded. What are called the *Maîtriſes* in France are much the ſame as the companies of towns corporate in England, only ſtill more injurious in their effects; as in England manufacturers may carry on many branches of workmanſhip out of the limits of the corporation, without having been made free of particular companies; whereas, in France, all tradeſmen are obliged to obtain the freedom of their proper maîtriſe, before they can ſet up any where. I know not whether this ill-judged regulation has been done away by the late revolution, but ſhould ſuppoſe it has, with many other abſurdities, been aboliſhed.

The

The obvious confequence of all reftrictions, fimilar to thofe of companies corporate, is the obftruction of the free circulation of labour. An individual who, from natural ingenuity or application, is qualified to exert any particular branch of induftry, cannot fix himfelf in a city, from fituation, perhaps, and other circumftances, the moft advantageous for his bufinefs; becaufe he has not ferved a tedious, and in many inftances, an unneceffary apprenticefhip, to an interefted inhabitant. All obftruction to the free circulation of labour is an impediment to the employment of the people; and we accordingly find, that commerce and manufactures have in general deferted thofe cities where fuch regulations are adhered to; and if any of fuch corporations ftill retain a confiderable fhare of bufinefs, it is principally, perhaps, to be attributed to fome advantages of fituation, conveniency of materials, or other encouraging circumftances. In England, the principal manufacturing towns are exempt from corporation reftrictions: as inftances, we may cite Manchefter, Leeds, Birmingham, and a confiderable portion of London, viz. Weftminfter, Southwark, and the fuburbs. In the

Auftrian

Auſtrian Netherlands, many of their cities are in a ſtate of depopulation from adherence to ſuch regulations; while the induſtrious have aſſembled in villages exempt from theſe reſtrictions, which begin to equal the former populouſneſs of the decayed bodies corporate.

In addition to corporation reſtrictions, which prevail in Great Britain as well as in the other parts of Europe, the free circulation of labour receives an additional obſtruction in England, from what are called the *Laws of Settlement*, which, though not connected with the corporation ſyſtems, may be ſlightly noticed. As ſuch laws are peculiar to England, a particular hiſtory of their origin and nature need not here be entered into; let a general ſketch ſuffice. Every pariſh in England, it is well known, is obliged to provide for the maintenance of its own poor: to render its burden as light as poſſible, each pariſh became anxious to prevent the inhabitants of any other pariſhes from ſettling in it, who might poſſibly be reduced to the neceſſity of throwing themſelves on its charity. To prevent ſuch migrations, and to confine as much as poſſible the different poor to the pariſhes in which they were born, the Laws of Settlement were deviſed; the general ſpirit and tendency of which, however they have been modified from time to time, is to confine the indigent labourer to the diſtrict in which he firſt chanced to enter on the labours and difficulties of this world, and to prevent him from forming a ſettlement elſewhere, however advantageous and inviting. Hence, principally, ariſes the very great irregularity in the price of labour, obſervable in many parts of England. The labourer is confined to his native ſoil; and though employment ſhould be overſtocked in one pariſh, and ill-ſupplied in another, the free circulation of labour being thus obſtructed, the inequality continues, to the general detriment both of the employer and the employed.

The impolicy of ſuch regulations, and of the corporation reſtrictions already noticed, and the impediments they occaſion to the employment of the people, are, I hope, ſufficiently obvious: their injuſtice is equally palpable. Ingenuity or corporal labour are the only ſources from which the

the indigent can derive ſubſiſtence and ſupport. To forbid the exertion of either, on any account, or in any ſituation, is as unjuſtiſiable as impolitic. It is depriving man of the ſource of ſuſtenance, beſtowed him by the Almighty. It is wreſting from him the moſt neceſſary, the moſt ſacred, and, one would imagine, the moſt inalienable of all rights, the right to labour.

Corporations are injurious to the induſtry and employment of the people, by levying taxes, tolls, and impoſitions on the ſeveral articles they bring to market. The freedom of internal commerce, as has already been obſerved, and as the moſt reſpectable authorities have acknowledged, is the principal ſource of the wealth, proſperity, and employment of the inhabitants of any empire: but how conſiderably muſt it be obſtructed by the levying of impoſitions, which are generally farmed out to the avaricious, indigent, or rapacious? Such impoſitions, when levied on the neceſſary articles of life, are productive of an additional evil; by raiſing their value, they diſtreſs the manufacturer, increaſe the price of his productions, diminiſh, of conſequence, their conſumption,

ſumption, and of courſe obſtruct the employment of thoſe engaged in them. But for what purpoſes were ſuch taxes levied? not in general for any public improvement, advantage, or convenience; for each of theſe a ſeparate tax is levied. Their amount is uſually ſquandered in diſſipation and luxury, the example of which is pernicious; or in ſupporting a number of drones, under the denomination of Aldermen and Magiſtrates, indolent from affluence, and bloated from exceſs. The government of any city needs no ſuch expedients; let its inhabitants elect a number of officers proportioned to its population and extent; let them aſſign them adequate, but not exorbitant ſalaries; and let the amount of ſuch ſalaries be levied, not from non-reſidents who ſupply them with neceſſaries; not by a mode which oppreſſes the feeble, obſtructs the commerce of the merchant, and impedes the employment of the people; but from thoſe to whom the protection is afforded, and by means unproductive of injury, injuſtice, and diſtreſs. Mancheſter gives an example of the inutility of corporation government: its inhabitants, amounting to above fifty thouſand, are governed by a magi-

ſtrate

ſtrate of no greater eminence than a conſtable, aſſiſted by inferior officers; and many other manufacturing towns in England are governed in a ſimilar way.

Excluſive Mercantile Companies, as Smith very juſtly obſerves, "reſemble in every reſpect the "corporations of trades, ſo common in the cities "and towns of all the countries of Europe; "and are a ſort of enlarged monopolies of the "ſame kind. As no inhabitant of a town can "exerciſe an incorporated trade, without firſt "obtaining his freedom in the corporation; ſo, "in moſt caſes, no ſubject of the ſtate can law-"fully carry on any branch of foreign trade, "for which a regulated company is eſtabliſhed, "without firſt becoming a member of that com-"pany." As ſuch companies are the ſame in their nature, with companies corporate, their views, motives, and conduct are generally ſimilar: their profits ariſe from the loſſes of the public; they contrive to export a ſmall quantity of native manufactures, in order to ſell them at an extravagant price; and they import a ſimilar ſupply of foreign produce, on which, competition being excluded,

excluded, they obtain an exorbitant profit at home. Their charter effectually excludes such competition, and the public are necessitated to acquiesce in the extortion. Beside, how unjust is it to exclude nine thousand nine hundred and ninety-nine out of ten thousand industrious subjects from different branches of trade, in which they might find useful occupation themselves, and afford it to others. This, however, is the effect of the East India charter in England; nay, its effects have, by the collusion of our own government, been extended to this unfortunate country. By the Turkey company charter thousands are shut out from any intercourse with the whole Turkish empire; and the conduct of its members has been such, that besides preventing others from reaping any benefit from the Levant trade their own commerce has sunk and declined, while that of France with the same countries has risen in proportion with the declension of its rival. Of this Marseilles affords convincing proofs.

Unfortunate, indeed, has been the general fate of all exclusive mercantile monopolies: such has been the ſhort-ſightedneſs, avarice, and miſmanagement of their members, that by far the greater number have at length failed; and thoſe that remain are more indebted for the prolongation of their exiſtence to the aſſiſtance and interference of their reſpective governments than to their own prudence and reſources: witneſs the Eaſt India company of England. The Abbé Morellet has given a liſt of fifty-five excluſive companies for foreign trade, which have been formed in different parts of Europe ſince the year 1600; every one of which have failed, notwithſtanding their particular privileges. The only pretext, therefore, which can be offered for their formation and continuance, viz. that they are neceſſary for conducting a trade with many countries, from the inability of individuals to effect it, falls to the ground. On the contrary, they have always injured and ruined the commerce committed to them: they have checked the induſtry and employment of many individuals, who would otherwiſe have ſucceſsfully engaged in it; and we may, therefore, ſafely conclude, in the words of Smith, "that all excluſive companies are nui-"ſances in every reſpect."

Such

Such appear to be the principal of the impediments to the induſtry and employment of the people, which the policy of the European governments has occaſioned: many, no doubt, exiſt, which we have not particularly noticed; but they may be eaſily referred to one or other of the claſſes above ſpecified, and their injurious tendency explained on ſome of the general principles we have attempted to eſtabliſh. Many others, alſo, of conſiderable efficacy, are neceſſarily deferred to the third ſection of the preſent part of our ſubject, which we ſhall now proceed to conſider, and inquire what is the ſyſtem of induſtry moſt beneficial to be purſued, and moſt productive of employment to the people at large.

SECTION III.

On the Syſtem of Induſtry moſt beneficial to be purſued, and moſt productive of Employment to the People at large.

Two general ſyſtems of induſtry and employment— I. The ſyſtem of commerce—Its two great engines—Reſtraints on importation of two kinds— 1ſt, The firſt ſpecies do not increaſe the general induſtry or employment of a people—The induſtry and employment muſt be proportioned to the capital of a people—Theſe regulations of the commercial ſyſtem diminiſh the general capital— Proofs of this—Such regulations may prematurely eſtabliſh manufactures; but this, inſtead of increaſing, will diminiſh the general capital—Two caſes in which ſuch regulations may be uſeful— 1. The regulations of the commercial ſyſtem under conſideration ſhould be altered with caution—2. The ſecond head of the regulations of the commercial ſyſtem, more abſurd even than the firſt —They diminiſh the general capital of a people —Preference

—Preference of markets no sound reason for these regulations—The whole doctrine on which they are founded absurd—Difference between balance of trade and balance of produce and consumption—Unnecessary to consider the other regulations of the commercial system—The inventors and supporters of the commercial system—II. *System of agriculture—Its outlines—Three classes of the people*—1. *Proprietors*—2. *Farmers are the only productive class*—3. *Artificers are unproductive, and why—Are maintained by the others—Yet still are useful—To discourage merchants or mercantile states impolitic—Freedom of trade the most advantageous mode of raising up manufacturers, and why—Effects of a contrary plan—Capital error of this system—The most just which has been published—Considerable alterations in favour of the agricultural system not to be expected—Still these discussions are useful—Further arguments in favour of agriculture—It increases the general capital more than any other business, and therefore general employment—It employs more numbers, directly, and indirectly—It secures employment more effectually—Proofs of this, from an*

an historic view of the Netherlands, and of Lombardy and Tuscany—Eulogium of Raynal on agriculture—The encouragement of manufactures promotes agriculture, and should therefore claim peculiar attention—Conclusion.

SECTION III.

IT need ſcarcely be repeated, that the ſyſtem of induſtry moſt advantageous to be purſued by any country muſt vary with its natural products and ſituation, its progreſs in civilization, its political defects and advantages, and a thouſand minutiæ not neceſſary to be here enumerated. In conſidering this, however, as well as the preceding ſubjects, ſome general principles may be eſtabliſhed, which will aſſiſt our inquiries when directed to any particular people, and which will apply to moſt nations, however different in ſoil, products, political, or other circumſtances.

In endeavouring to form ſome concluſion upon this comprehenſive ſubject, the Eſſayiſt is in a great degree aſſiſted by having his views neceſſarily confined to the conſideration of the two grand ſyſtems of induſtry and employment which have been purſued by man, viz. *The Syſtem of Commerce* and *The Syſtem of Agriculture.*

ture. Thefe two fyftems, which, as we fhall endeavour to fhew, fhould in general go hand-in-hand, have been fo far feparated and fet in oppofition to each other, that the former has pretty generally, and, in modern European ftates, has almoft univerfally been affifted, protected, and fupported, at the expence of the latter. The nature of thefe two different fyftems of induftry, and the relative importance of each, as far as refpects the employment of the people, we fhall now proceed to explain; and, in doing fo, fhall have frequent recourfe to that invaluable political performance, the Inquiry of Dr. Smith. He has explained, in fo clear and juft a manner, every circumftance relating to thefe two fyftems of induftry, that I fhall frequently take the liberty of copying his words, diftinguifhing them only by inverted commas: his illuftration of the fubject it would be prefumption to attempt improving on; his fentiments cannot be better conveyed than in his own fimple, yet forcible ftile.

I. The *Syftem of Commerce,* which includes manufactures, and which prevails univerfally in

Europe,

Europe, affects to enrich the inhabitants of any nation, as well as to afford them employment, by procuring what is called a favourable balance of trade; or " by exporting to a greater value " than its import: the great object, therefore, of " this system of political œconomy is to dimi- " nish as much as possible the importation of " foreign goods for home consumption, and to " increase as much as possible the exportation of " the produce of domestic industry.—Its two " great engines for effecting these purposes are, " *restraints* upon importation, and *encouragement* " to exportation."—The former, as more connected with the present subject, we shall chiefly consider here; and the discussion of its merits will almost equally well apply to the other general expedients of the system of commerce.— " Restraints upon importation are of two kinds; " 1. Restaints upon the importation of such fo- " reign goods for home consumption as could " be produced at home, from whatever country " they are imported; and, 2. Restraints upon " the importation of goods of almost all kinds, " from those particular countries with which the " balance of trade is supposed to be disadvan- " tageous."

" tageous." That the wealth of nations does not confiſt in an imaginary balance of trade in its favour, but in the real value of the annual produce of the land and labour of its inhabitants, has by Dr. Smith been ſo fully ſhewn, that any particular recapitulation of his arguments would be here unneceſſary: the reſtrictions of the commercial ſyſtem, if intended for this purpoſe, are, therefore, nugatory. Let us ſee if they tend to increaſe the general induſtry, or to promote the general employment of the people.

Reſtraining by high duties, or totally preventing by prohibitions, the importation of ſuch articles as are produced or manufactured by the natives of particular countries, neceſſarily ſecures to them, in a greater or leſs degree, the monopoly of the home market for ſuch articles. That ſuch a monopoly encourages the particular ſpecies of employment, in favour of which it is eſtabliſhed, cannot admit of a doubt: it is very doubtful, however, whether it increaſes the *general* induſtry of a nation, or promotes the *general* employment of its natives. The general induſtry and employment of a people muſt always

be

be proportioned to the amount of the capital they are poſſeſſed of; as the number of journeymen kept by a maſter manufacturer muſt be determined by the amount of the capital he employs in his particular branch of buſineſs. The capital of a people is the aggregate of the capital of all the individuals which compoſe a nation. A variety of reſtrictions, regulations, and monopolies, may direct a greater part of this capital towards ſome particular branches of buſineſs, than they would naturally have attracted if things were allowed to find their natural level: but if ſuch regulations and monopolies cannot increaſe the *general* capital of a nation, they cannot increaſe the *general* induſtry, or promote the *general* employment of a people. That the general capital of a people cannot be increaſed by meaſures of this nature, but, on the contrary, muſt be diminiſhed, is evident from very obvious conſiderations.

Every individual employed in buſineſs naturally endeavours to diſcover the moſt beneficial mode of employing, and conſequently the moſt effectual mode of increaſing, his capital. If no particular

particular branches of induſtry were encouraged more than others, thoſe would naturally be preferred which afforded the ſpeedieſt means of increaſing the particular capital of individuals, and conſequently the general capital of a people. It is ſelf-intereſt which would direct man in this as in almoſt every other inſtance; but the ſtudy of this intereſt would in the preſent, as in many other inſtances, neceſſarily lead him to the moſt effectual means of promoting the intereſts of ſociety at large. The individual muſt neceſſarily be ſuppoſed better able to judge what particular branch of induſtry is beſt calculated for his capital and ſituation, and moſt likely to augment that capital, than any ſtateſman or law-giver whatever. It would be deemed extremely iniquitous in any branch of any legiſlature to interfere directly in a man's private concerns, and aſſume the power of obliging him to employ his capital in that buſineſs only which the legiſlature deemed moſt advantageous for him. By the eſtabliſhment of monopolies, and the other mercantile reſtrictions, however, a ſimilar power has been in ſome meaſure indirectly carried into execution. To give the monopoly of the home market

market to the produce of any art or manufacture, is to direct the people to employ more capital in that way than they otherwise would have done; and muft be a regulation, either ufelefs or pernicious: if the produce of domeftic employment can be brought to market as cheap as that of foreign, it is certainly an ufelefs regulation: the advantages of the goods being expofed to fale, free of the charges of freight, commiffion, and infurance, and the difadvantages of employing capital at a diftance, to which foreign goods muft be liable, would appear fufficient encouragement to domeftic produce. If, on the contrary, foreign produce can be brought to market cheaper than home, the regulation is pernicious, as neceffarily diminifhing the general capital of a country. A mafter of a family never attempts to manufacture at home what it will coft him more to manufacture than to purchafe. The tailor will not make the fhoes his family may wear, but buys them from the fhoemaker; the fhoemaker will not make his own clothes, but employs the tailor: every individual, in fhort, finds it tend more to his advantage, and to the increafe of his capital, to buy the different

ferent

ferent articles he has occasion for from the cheapest market, than to manufacture them at home, at an ultimately dearer rate. "What is prudence in "the conduct of a private family can scarcely be "folly in a great kingdom." If foreigners can supply us with different articles at a cheaper rate than our own manufacturers, it is better to purchase at a cheap rate from the former than at an exorbitant price from the latter. The general industry of a country would not suffer, as may be supposed, by such a procedure. The capital employed in these branches of industry would be left to find out some other direction, more beneficial to society at large; more beneficial, because the *general* capital of society, and, consequently, the *general* fund for employment, must be diminished by their being obliged to purchase different articles at a dearer rate than they could otherwise obtain them, in proportion to the excess of price of the domestic, over the foreign object of purchase.

By regulations of this nature, indeed, particular manufactures may be established in a country sooner than they would if every branch of employment

employment was left to find its natural level; and, in time, their products may be afforded as cheap, or perhaps cheaper, than foreign goods of the ſame kind. But it by no means follows, that the general capital and fund of employment would be increaſed by ſuch a meaſure. On the contrary, that fund, and conſequently the general induſtry and employment of the inhabitants of any country, muſt be diminiſhed by the increaſed price they are neceſſitated to pay for articles which could be obtained cheaper elſewhere. Nor is it by any means certain, that the advantages which may ultimately ariſe from thus forcing a manufacture, will counterbalance the certain loſs ſuch an eſtabliſhment of them muſt at firſt occaſion. Its immediate effect muſt be, to diminiſh the revenue and capital of a country; and any cauſe of ſuch diminution, is not likely to encreaſe that capital faſter than it would naturally have augmented of its own accord. Though for want of ſuch regulations ſociety ſhould never acquire the propoſed manufacture, it would not on that account neceſſarily be the poorer in any one period of its duration. In every period of its duration its whole capital and industry might still have been employed, though upon different objects, in the manner that was most advantageous at the time. In every period its revenue might have been the greatest its capital could afford, and both might have been augmented with the greatest possible rapidity.

" The natural advantages which one country " has over another, in producing particular com- " modities, are sometimes so great, that it is ac- " knowledged by all the world to be in vain to " struggle with them. By means of glasses, hot " beds, and hot walls, very good grapes can " be raised in Scotland, and very good wine " too can be made of them, at about thirty times " the expence, for which at least equally good " can be brought from foreign countries. Would " it be a reasonable law to prohibit the impor- " tation of foreign wines, merely to encourage " the making of Claret and Burgundy in Scot- " land? But if there would be a manifest ab- " surdity in turning towards any employment " thirty times more of the capital and indus- " try of the country than would be necessary to " purchase from foreign countries an equal quan- " tity of the commodities wanted, there must

" be

" be an abſurdity, though not altogether ſo glar-
" ing, yet exactly of the ſame kind, in turning
" towards any ſuch employment a thirtieth, or
" even a three hundredth part more, of either.
" Whether the advantages which one country
" has over another be natural or acquired, is,
" in this reſpect, of no conſequence. As long as
" the one country has thoſe advantages, and the
" other wants them, it will always be more
" advantageous for the latter rather to buy of
" the former, than to make. It is an acquired
" advantage only which one artificer has over his
" neighbour who exerciſes another trade, and
" yet they both find it more advantageous to
" buy of one another than to make what does
" not belong to their reſpective trades."

There are two caſes, according to Smith, in which it may be advantageous to impoſe taxes and reſtrictions upon foreign, in favour of domeſtic, induſtry. Firſt, when the encouragement of ſome particular ſort of employment is neceſſary for the defence of a country; as that of maritime employment is to Great Britain. The act of navigation, therefore, as it gives a monopoly of the carrying trade of Great Britain to her own ſailors, is, in her, a politic meaſure; as it neceſſarily increaſes their number, and conſequently the naval ſtrength of the nation. Secondly, It may be advantageous to tax any branch of foreign, in favour of a ſimilar ſpecies of domeſtic, induſtry, when a tax is impoſed at home upon the latter. This would be only reducing each to a ſtate of equality, and would not direct a greater ſhare of domeſtic ſtock and induſtry to that particular employment than it would naturally have attracted. When foreign nations alſo prohibit the importation of ſome of our goods into their dominions, it may be a matter of deliberation, whether we ſhould not retaliate by loading theirs with ſimilar impoſts. Revenge naturally dictates ſuch procedure, and we find that nations have generally obeyed its dictates. If ſuch retaliation will occaſion a repeal of the obnoxious duties and impoſitions, in the foreign country, it will be adviſeable to adopt and perſiſt in it; if not, it is ſurely impolitic to redreſs an injury done to one ſet of manufacturers in a country, by injuring all the other members of the community, which is ne-

ceſſarily

ceſſarily the conſequence of prohibiting the foreign produce of a ſimilar, and, perhaps, of many other manufactures, and obliging the people to purchaſe them at a dearer rate from domeſtic or other workmen.

When by the long eſtabliſhment of reſtrictions upon importation, and by the monopoly of the home market, a conſiderable number of hands are employed in any particular manufacture, it would require conſiderable caution and circumſpection to deprive them of ſuch protection and monopoly, by throwing open the home market to ſimilar foreign produce. It would be unjuſt to deprive numbers of the ſource of employment which they have made the ſtudy of their lives, in the confidence that that market for their labours was fully ſecured to them. Cheaper foreign articles might, in conſequence, be poured in ſo faſt, as to deprive thouſands all at once of employment and ſupport.

The diſorder, however, occaſioned by adopting ſuch a meaſure, would probably be leſs conſiderable than at firſt view might be imagined.

When any particular branch of manufacture has been eſtabliſhed for a ſeries of years in a country, the acquired advantages of the manufacturer in that branch become ſo conſiderable, that they alone would, in moſt inſtances, ſecure to him the home market againſt any foreign competition. The ſilk manufacture is, perhaps, the principal exception to this obſervation in England; and this is chiefly occaſioned by the diſadvantages they labour under in importing the primum of the manufacture. Another circumſtance, which would conſiderably diminiſh the diſorder and diſtreſs apprehended from ſuch a meaſure, is, that the greater number of the hands engaged in the manufactures ſo left unprotected, would, in caſe of their declenſion, find employment in ſome other line. At the cloſe of a war thouſands of ſailors and ſoldiers are diſbanded, and deprived, we may ſay, of their trade; yet, in a ſhort time, they ſpread over the country, and find employment for themſelves in a variety of other occupations.

The next head of the reſtraints, adopted by the commercial ſyſtem, are thoſe upon the importation

portation of almoſt all kind of articles, from thoſe countries with whom the balance of trade is ſuppoſed to be diſadvantageous. Theſe are even more abſurd than thoſe we have been conſidering, and tend equally to diminiſh the employment of the inhabitants of any nation by whom they are adopted. That any diminution of the capital of a country neceſſarily diminiſhes the employment of its inhabitants we have already ſhewn. That the reſtrictions, now under conſideration, prevent that capital from accumulating to ſo conſiderable an amount, as it naturally would, were the commerce of a country allowed to take a ſpontaneous direction, may be briefly demonſtrated.

Although it were certain, in the firſt place, that what has been called the balance of trade between any two countries, ſuppoſing their commerce free from all reſtrictions, was in favour of one of them, it by no means follows that the trade with ſuch a nation would be unfavourable to the other; or that the *general* balance of its commerce would be thereby turned more againſt itſelf than if the uſual reſtrictions on importa-

tion

tion were adopted. On the contrary, "if the "wines of France, for example, are better and "cheaper than thoſe of Portugal, or its linens "than thoſe of Germany, it would be more "advantageous for Great Britain to purchaſe "both the wine and the foreign linen which it "has occaſion for, from France, than of Por- "tugal and Germany; though the value of "the annual importations from France would be "thereby greatly augmented," and the amount of the apparent balance of trade in its favour increaſed, "the value of the *whole* annual im- "portations" into Great Britain "would be "diminiſhed, in proportion as the French goods "of the ſame quality were cheaper than thoſe "of the other two countries;" and of conſe- quence the general capital of Great Britain, the general fund for the employment of all its inha- bitants, would be increaſed in proportion to the ſum ſaved by purchaſing certain articles cheap in one country rather than dear in another.

It has been adopted, indeed, as a maxim, that becauſe ſome countries give others a preference of their home market for different articles, a

ſimilar

ſimilar favour and encouragement ſhould be afforded them in return. The Portugueſe were better cuſtomers for the manufactures of Great Britain than the French; and therefore the dear and bad wines of the former country were to be preferred to the cheap and good liquors of the latter. As one nation gives us *their* cuſtom, we, it is aſſerted, ſhould give them *ours*. "The "ſneaking arts of underling tradeſmen are thus "erected into political maxims for the conduct "of a great empire: for it is the moſt under-"ling tradeſmen only who make it a rule chiefly "to employ their own cuſtomers. A great "trader purchaſes his goods always where they "are cheapeſt and beſt, without regard to any "little intereſt of this kind."

But, in the ſecond place, "nothing can be "more abſurd than this whole doctrine of the "balance of trade, upon which not only theſe "reſtraints, but almoſt all the other regulations "of commerce, are founded. When two places "trade with each other, this doctrine ſuppoſes "that if the balance be even, neither of them "either loſes or gains; but if it leans in any

"degree

" degree to one ſide, that one of them loſes, " and the other gains, in proportion to its de- " clenſion from the juſt equilibrium. Both ſup- " poſitions are falſe: for by advantage or gain " is to be underſtood, not the increaſe, or the " quantity of gold and ſilver, but that of the " exchangeable value of the annual produce of " the land and labour of the country, or the " increaſe of the annual revenue of its inhabi- " tants. If the balance be even, and if the " trade between the two places conſiſt altoge- " ther in the exchange of their native commo- " dities, they will, upon moſt occaſions, not only " both gain, but they will gain equally: each " will in this caſe afford a market for a part " of the ſurplus produce of the other; each " will replace a capital which had been em- " ployed in raiſing and preparing for the market " this part of the ſurplus produce of the other, " and which had been diſtributed among, and " given revenue, maintenance," and employ- ment to a certain number of its inhabitants. Some part of the inhabitants of each, therefore, will derive their revenue, maintenance, and em- ployment, from the other.

There

There is another balance, indeed, very different from the balance of trade; and which, according as it happens to be favourable or unfavourable, neceſſarily occaſions the proſperity or decay of every nation. This is the balance of the annual produce and conſumption. If the exchangeable value of the annual produce exceeds that of the annual conſumption, the capital of the ſociety muſt annually increaſe in proportion to this exceſs. If the exchangeable value of the annual produce, on the contrary, fall ſhort of the annual conſumption, the capital of the ſociety muſt annually decay in proportion to this deficiency. The expence of the ſociety in this caſe exceeds its revenue, and neceſſarily encroaches upon its capital: its capital, therefore, muſt neceſſarily decay, and with it the exchangeable value of the annual produce of its induſtry. This balance of produce and conſumption is entirely different from what is called the balance of trade. The balance of produce and conſumption may be conſtantly in favour of a nation, when what is called the balance of trade is againſt it: a nation may export to a greater value than it imports, for half a century, perhaps,

together;

together; the gold and ſilver which comes into it, during all this time, may be all immediately ſent out of it; its circulating coin may gradually decay; different ſorts of paper money being ſubſtituted in its place; and even the debts, too, which it contracts in the different nations with whom it deals, may be gradually increaſing; and yet its real wealth, the exchangeable value of the annual produce of its lands and labour, "its capital, and the fund for the em-"ployment of its people," may, during the ſame period, have been increaſing in a much greater proportion. The ſtate of North America, and of its trade with the reſt of the world, "may ſerve as a proof that this is by "no means an impoſſible ſuppoſition."

It were needleſs here particularly to inſiſt upon the other expedients which have been had recourſe to, for aſſiſting and ſupporting the commercial ſyſtem; ſuch as the eſtabliſhment of colonies, the monopolizing their trade, and the giving them the monopoly of the home market for their produce; the eſtabliſhment of bounties for the encouragement of infant manufac-

tures,

tures, and the various other ſubordinate devices of this complicated ſyſtem of employment. Thoſe who wiſh for more particular information on ſuch ſubjects, we have only again to refer to Doctor Smith's ineſtimable treatiſe on The Wealth of Nations. He has fully ſhewn, that all theſe regulations and reſtrictions uſually diminiſh, in a greater or leſs degree, the general wealth and capital of a nation; their effects, however, in diminiſhing the general employment of a people, will ever be proportionate to their efficacy in diminiſhing that capital, which is the principal ſource and fund for labour and employment.

It is no difficult matter to determine, who were the inventors, and who are the principal advocates and ſupporters of a ſyſtem, which augments the riches and aſſiſts the induſtry of a *few* inhabitants of a nation, at the expence of the *many*, and to the depreſſion and obſtruction of the general induſtry and employment of the majority. They were and are the merchants and manufacturers, who have been too ſucceſsful in perſuading every country in Europe, that the wealth of every nation, and the employment of its natives,

tives, depended principally upon aggrandizing *them*, at the expence of every other inhabitant of the ſtate. To carry their views into execution, to elevate their branch of induſtry above the level of every other, the man of landed property, the cultivator of the ſoil, the working labourer in almoſt every department of buſineſs, the great majority, in ſhort, of every European nation, have ſubmitted to monopolies, reſtrictions, and prohibitions without number, whoſe ultimate effect has been, to raiſe the price of the natural and artificial neceſſaries of life beyond what they would otherwiſe have attained, and conſequently to diminiſh the general clear revenue and capital of every people, the only true fund for their labour, and permanent ſource of their employment.

II. *The Syſtem of Agriculture*, which we ſhall now briefly explain, is one which has exiſted rather in theory than practice: it is the offspring of the ſpeculation of a few learned and ingenious Frenchmen, and has never, in its full extent, been carried into execution by any nation. The commerce and manufactures of France, having,

by

by the regulations of her famous minifter Colbert, obtained a more than ordinary preference and pre-eminence over its agriculture, the difcouragement and depreffion this latter branch of induftry experienced was fuch as to be felt in a greater or lefs degree by every inhabitant of the country. To difcover the caufes of the confequent diftrefs, different inquiries were fet on foot; and one of the principal was difcovered to be the preference given by the inftitutions of Colbert to the manufacturing above the agricultural interefts. This gave rife to the publications of M. Quefnai, the profound author of the agricultural fyftem: he has been followed by many ingenious difciples, who have been diftinguifhed as a fect by the title of *Oeconomifts*; and who ever exprefs the greateft admiration and reverence for their mafter. The general outlines of the fyftem are briefly thefe:

" The different orders of the people, who have ever been fuppofed to contribute in any refpect towards the annual produce of the land and labour of the country, they divide into three claffes. The firft is the clafs of the proprietors of land.

land. The ſecond is the claſs of the cultivators, of farmers and country labourers, whom they honour with the peculiar appellation of *the productive claſs*. The third is the claſs of artificers, manufacturers, and merchants, whom they endeavour to degrade by the humiliating appellation of the *barren* or *unproductive claſs*.

The claſs of proprietors contributes to the annual produce, by the expence which they may occaſionally lay out upon the improvement of the land, upon the buildings, drains, encloſures, and other ameliorations, which they may either make or maintain upon it; and, by means of which the cultivators are enabled with the ſame capital to raiſe a greater produce, and, conſequently, to pay a greater rent. Such expences are called ground expences, *dépenſes foncieres*.

The cultivators or farmers contribute to the annual produce by what are, in this ſyſtem, called the original and annual expences, *dépenſes primitives annuelles*; which they lay out upon the cultivation of the land. Thoſe two ſorts of expences are two capitals, which the farmer employs in cultivation; and unleſs they are regularly reſtored

ſtored to him, together with a reaſonable profit, he cannot carry on his employment upon a level with other employments ; but, from a regard to his own intereſt, muſt deſert it as ſoon as poſſible, and ſeek ſome other. The rent, which properly belongs to the landlord, is no more than the neat produce which remains after paying in the completeſt manner all the expences which muſt be neceſſarily laid out, in order to raiſe the groſs or the whole produce. It is becauſe the labour of the cultivators, over and above paying completely all theſe neceſſary expences, affords a neat produce of this kind, the rent, that this claſs of people are, in this ſyſtem, peculiarly diſtinguiſhed by the honourable appellation of the productive claſs.

Artificers and manufacturers, whoſe induſtry, in the common apprehenſions of men, increaſes ſo much the value of the rude produce of land, are in this ſyſtem repreſented as a ſet of people altogether barren and unproductive: their labour, it is ſaid, replaces only the ſtock which employs them, together with its ordinary profits. The profits of manufacturing ſtock are not, like the

the rent of land, a neat produce, which remains after completely repaying the whole of the expence which muſt be laid out in order to obtain them. The ſtock of the farmer yields him a profit, as well as that of the maſter manufacturer; and it yields a rent likewiſe to another perſon, which that of the maſter manufacturer does not. Mercantile ſtock is, for the ſame reaſons, equally barren and unproductive with manufacturing ſtock. Artificers, manufacturers, and merchants, can augment the revenue and wealth of their ſociety by parſimony only, or, as it is expreſſed in this ſyſtem, by *privation*. Farmers and country labourers, on the contrary, may enjoy completely the whole profits of their ſtock, the whole funds of their ſubſiſtence, and yet augment at the ſame time the revenue and wealth of ſociety.

The unproductive claſs, that of merchants, artificers, and manufacturers, is maintained and employed altogether at the expence of the two other claſſes, that of the proprietors and that of cultivators. They furniſh it both with the materials of its work, and with the fund of its ſubſiſtence;

fubfiftence; with the corn and cattle which it confumes, while it is employed about that work. The proprietors and cultivators, finally, pay both the wages of all the workmen of the unproductive clafs, and the profits of all their employers. Thofe workmen and their employers are properly the fervants of the proprietors and cultivators; they are only fervants which work without doors, as menial fervants work within.

The unproductive clafs is not only ufeful, but greatly ufeful to the other two claffes: by means of the induftry of merchants, artificers and manufacturers, the proprietors and cultivators can purchafe both the foreign goods, and the manufactured produce of their own country, which they have occafion for, with the produce of a much fmaller quantity of their own labour than what they would be obliged to employ if they were to attempt, in an awkward and unfkilful manner, either to import the one, or to make the other for their own ufe. It can never be the intereft of the proprietors and cultivators to reftrain or to difcourage in any refpect the induftry of merchants, artificers, or manufacturers. The merchants, artificers and manufacturers of those mercantile ſtates, which, like Holland and Hamburgh, conſiſt chiefly of this unproductive claſs, are in the ſame manner maintained and employed altogether at the expence of the proprietors and cultivators of land.

It can never be the intereſt of the landed nations who ſupport them to diſcourage or diſtreſs the induſtry of ſuch mercantile ſtates, by impoſing high duties upon their trade, or upon the commodities which they furniſh. Such duties, by rendering thoſe commodities dearer, could ſerve only to ſink the real value of the ſurplus produce of their own land, with which, or, what comes to the ſame thing, with the price of which, thoſe commodities are purchaſed. The moſt effectual expedient, on the contrary, for raiſing the value of that ſurplus produce, for encouraging the increaſe, and conſequently the cultivation and improvement of their own land, would be to allow the moſt perfect freedom to the trade of all ſuch mercantile nations.

This perfect freedom of trade would even be the most effectual expedient for supplying them, in due time, with all the artificers, manufacturers, and merchants, whom they wanted at home; and for filling up, in the properest and most advantageous manner, that very important void which they left there.

The continual increase of the surplus produce of their land would, in due time, create a greater capital than what could be employed with the ordinary rate of profit in the improvement and cultivation of land; and the surplus part of it would naturally turn itself to the employment of artificers and manufacturers at home. But those artificers and manufacturers, finding at home both the materials of their work and the fund of their subsistence, might immediately, even with much less art and skill, be able to work as cheap as the like artificers and manufacturers of such mercantile states, who had *both* to bring from a great distance. These latter would, therefore, immediately be rivalled in the market of those landed nations, and soon after undersold, and jostled out of it altogether. The cheapnefs of the manufactures of thofe landed nations, in confequence of the gradual improvements of art and fkill, would, in due time, extend their fale beyond the home market, and carry them to many foreign markets, from which they would in the fame manner gradually joftle out many of the manufactures of fuch mercantile nations.

According to this liberal and generous fyftem, therefore, the moft advantageous method in which a landed nation can raife up artificers, manufacturers, and merchants of its own, is, to grant the moft perfect freedom of trade to the artificers, manufacturers and merchants of all other nations. It thereby raifes the value of the furplus produce of its own land, of which the continual increafe gradually eftablifhes a fund, which in due time neceffarily raifes up all the artificers, merchants and manufacturers it has occafion for.

When a landed nation, on the contrary, oppreffes, either by high duties or by prohibitions, the trade of foreign nations, it neceffarily hurts its own intereft in two different ways. Firft, by raifing raiſing the price of all foreign goods, and of all ſorts of manufactures, it neceſſarily ſinks the real value of the ſurplus produce of its own land, with which, or, what comes to the ſame thing, with the price of which, it purchaſes thoſe foreign goods and manufactures. Secondly, by giving a ſort of monopoly of the home market to its own merchants, artificers, and manufacturers, it raiſes the rate of mercantile and manufacturing profit in proportion to that of agricultural profit, and conſequently either draws from agriculture a part of the capital which had before been employed in it, or hinders from going to it a part of what would otherwiſe have been ſo employed.

Though by this oppreſſive policy a landed nation *ſhould* even be able to raiſe up artificers, manufacturers and merchants of its own, ſomewhat ſooner than it could do by the freedom of trade; (a matter, however, which is not a little doubtful) yet it would raiſe them up, if one may ſay ſo, prematurely, and before it was perfectly ripe for them. By raiſing up too haſtily one ſpecies of induſtry, it would depreſs another

another more valuable ſpecies of induſtry; it would depreſs productive labour, by encouraging too haſtily that labour which is altogether barren and unproductive."

Such are the mere outlines of this very ingenious ſyſtem; the capital error of which appears to lie in its repreſenting the claſs of artificers, manufacturers and merchants, as altogether barren and unproductive. For many reaſons, however, this repreſentation is unjuſt, which may be more particularly examined in Doctor Smith's performance; but, with theſe imperfections, he heſitates not to pronounce, "that this ſyſtem is the neareſt approximation "to the truth that has yet been publiſhed upon "the ſubject of political œconomy; and that "it is upon that account well worth the con-"ſideration of every man, who wiſhes to exa-"mine with attention the principles of that very "important ſcience."

The above comparative ſtatement of the two grand ſyſtems of induſtry has been principally abbreviated from Doctor Smith, to whoſe work we muſt again refer for more particular information reſpecting them. Conſiderable inſight into each will alſo be acquired by conſulting a late work, intitled, " New and Old Principles " of Trade compared; or, a Treatiſe on the " Principles of Commerce between Nations *." The French writers on the ſubject may alſo be had recourſe to with advantage.

The arguments advanced would ſeem ſufficient to prove the injuſtice and impolicy of the reſtrictions by which the commercial ſyſtem has been extended and ſupported, at the expence, and to the prejudice, of the agricultural. To expect, indeed, that the governors of mankind will be prevailed upon by any arguments to remove theſe reſtrictions and oppreſſions, and to reſtore the different ſources of employment to their natural level and equality, would be an expectation truly vain and chimerical. The prejudices eſtabliſhed by old and familiar modes of reaſoning are againſt it. The numbers engaged in mercantile and manufacturing purſuits, and whoſe

* Publiſhed by Johnſon, London, 1789, 8vo.

whose profits principally depend on the monopolies which have been established, are too considerable to be injured with impunity, as they certainly would be by any considerable innovation. The revenue and very existence of some states has been so interwoven with these establishments, that they could scarcely be altered without confusion, distress, and bankruptcy. The capital which has been accumulated by mercantile engagements, not finding any other equally beneficial direction, has, for some time, in several countries, been daily laid out in agricultural improvements; and thus, what should have been the first step in the progress of nations, is reserved for the last. But, as the proverb says, "it is better late than never." Suddenly to shut the sources of that capital, which is thus finding its way to the country, may be ruinous both to the agricultural and manufacturing interests. Innumerable reasons, in short, occur, why such an alteration of system cannot be expected to take place in the states of Europe as at present constituted; but flourishing and stable will be the nations who first disengage themselves from such thraldrom. Secure, extensive,

and

and universally beneficial will be the employment of their people. America must strike the contemplation of any writer engaged in the consideration of these subjects. She has successfully thrown off the trammels of colonial restrictions; let her take heed to form no new ones for herself; let her know no such term as a *favoured nation*; let her ports be free to all people, as the winds which waft their vessels to her coasts; let her be deaf to the clamours of her merchants and manufacturers, should they solicit protection, and restraints. Manufactures will undoubtedly arise among her sons; but let them be the offspring of the natural progress to opulence, not the forced and hot-bed productions of monopoly.

But although the situation of Europe is at present such that we are not to expect the revolution in mercantile regulations alluded to; discussions of this nature will have their value, if they check the legislatures of different countries in granting any new monopolies; if they persuade them cautiously to relax those which already subsist; and, above all, if they turn their

attention

attention to that branch of politics which has been too long, and too confiderably, neglected and undervalued. Nay, they have, in fome degree, produced that effect; the importance of agriculture is better known, and more univerfally acknowledged; and nations begin to think that it is as conducive to their intereft to cultivate their long-neglected acres at home, as to roam after wafte and uncultivated tracts abroad.

The confiderations which have been advanced, explain, it is hoped, fufficiently, the *relative* importance of agriculture to a nation. To evince that it is the principal and moft fecure fource of employment to the people, fome further arguments may be adduced.

As the abundance of capital is the principal fource of employment, and as agriculture tends more than any other branch of bufinefs to increafe the *general* capital of a country, it muft in the fame proportion more effectually promote the employment of a people. To prove that it does poffefs this tendency, the following confiderations

derations may be advanced, in addition to thoſe already offered.

" No equal capital puts into motion a greater
" quantity of *productive* labour than that of the
" farmer. Not only his labouring ſervants, but
" his labouring cattle, are productive labourers.
" In agriculture, too, nature labours along with
" man ; and though her labour coſts no expence,
" its produce has its value, as well as that of
" the moſt expenſive workmen. The moſt im-
" portant operations of agriculture ſeem intend-
" ed not ſo much to increaſe, though they do
" that too, as to direct the fertility of nature,
" towards the production of plants moſt profit-
" able to man. A field overgrown with briars
" and brambles may frequently produce as great
" a quantity of vegetables as the beſt culti-
" vated vineyard or corn field. Planting and
" tillage frequently regulate, more than they
" animate, the active fertility of nature ; and
" after all their labour, a great part of the work
" always remains to be done by her. The la-
" bourers and labouring cattle, therefore, em-
" ployed in agriculture, not only occaſion, like

" the

"the workmen in manufactures, the reproduc-
"tion of a value equal to their own consump-
"tion, or to the capital which employs them,
"together with its own profits, but of a much
"greater value. Over and above the capital
"of the farmer, and all its profits, they regu-
"larly occasion the reproduction of the rent of
"the landlord. This rent may be considered
"as the produce of those powers of nature,
"the use of which the landlord lends to the
"farmer. It is greater or smaller according to
"the supposed extent of these powers, or ac-
"cording, in other words, to the supposed fer-
"tility of the land. It is the work of nature
"which remains, after deducting and compen-
"sating every thing which can be regarded as
"the work of man. It is seldom less than a
"fourth, and frequently more than a third of
"the whole produce. No equal quantity of
"productive labour employed in manufactures
"can ever occasion so great a reproduction. In
"them, nature does nothing, man does all;
"and the reproduction must always be in pro-
"portion to the strength of the agents that
"occasion it. The capital employed in agricul-

"ture,

" ture, therefore, not only puts into motion a " greater quantity of productive labour, than " any equal capital employed in manufactures; " but in proportion, too, to the quantity of pro- " ductive labour it employs, it adds a much " greater value to the annual produce of the " land and labour of the country, to the real " wealth and revenue of its inhabitants. Of all " the ways in which a capital can be employed, " it is *by far the most advantageous* to the so- " ciety."

The numbers employed in agriculture, in such large countries as France and England, have by some writers been computed at half, by others at a third, by none less than a fifth, of the whole inhabitants of the country. Sir James Stewart calculates that the proportion is in England as twelve to nine. However calculations may differ, those occupied in the culture of the earth, at any rate, considerably exceed in number those employed in any other species of manual labour, and, most probably, those engaged in every other species of employment put together. This very circumstance, of its affording immediate occupation

tion to ſo conſiderable a multitude, ſhould entitle agriculture to the moſt marked encouragement, and is an additional reaſon why it is to be conſidered the greateſt and moſt important ſource of labour and employment.

Beſide the multitudes to whom the culture of the earth affords immediate employment, it indirectly gives occupation to many more, in a greater degree, than any other branch of labour whatever; for, inaſmuch as it is the moſt friendly of all to long life and population, it neceſſarily occaſions the greateſt demand for the artificial neceſſaries of exiſtence, and therefore indirectly employs more artiſts and manufacturers than any other.

Agriculture is not only the great ſource of employment to a people, but when carried to perfection, ſecures that employment more effectually than any other occupation whatever. Manufactures and commerce are not neceſſarily confined to any country, however vigorous and flouriſhing they may be at any one period. Taxes, oppreſſion, civil diſſentions, foreign war, and a thouſand

thousand other causes, may check, discourage, or totally annihilate them, and deprive its natives of those sources of employment which once engaged multitudes. To this ample testimony is borne by those once great commercial states, which at present exist only in name, and further proofs will, in time, be afforded by those at present oppressed and declining. When capital, on the contrary, is laid out in highly cultivating the earth, it not only affords extensive employment to the present, but secures it to future generations. Of both these circumstances, one country in Europe affords a demonstration. I mean the Austrian Netherlands; a brief review of the ancient and present state of which will prove the justice of the observation just now made, and the general utility of agriculture to a state. The facts I shall take from the history of the country, and the remarks of the most judicious travellers.

The Netherlands in general, and the province of Flanders in particular, though now cultivated and improved to the utmost, afforded at one period a very different prospect. The vast

forest

foreſt of Ardennes, of which ſome ſmall but ornamental remains ſtill continue, overſpread and rendered uſeleſs almoſt its whole extent. The Counts of Flanders were, on this account, ſtiled the Foreſters of Flanders. The country was, beſide, covered with marſhes and ſtagnant waters. The Scheld, unreſtrained by the hand of man, overflowed its level banks, deluged the neighbouring plains, and rendered them at once both deſolate and unhealthy. Agriculture has effected the wonderful change now obſervable: introduced firſt by the Monks, and adopted afterwards by the peaſants, it made rapid advances to perfection, in proportion as the latter were relieved from the feodal oppreſſion, and ſecured from the rapacity of their lords. The manufactures afterwards eſtabliſhed in the cities of Flanders afforded additional encouragement to the cultivation of the country. They doubly promoted its progreſs to perfection: the huſbandman, ſecure of a ready market for his productions, in the riſing conſumption of the crowded towns, was invited to increaſe his exertions; and, by augmenting his capital, was enabled more effectually to execute the neceſſary improvements

provements in his farm. The adventurous merchant, not finding ſufficient ſcope for the employment of his wealth in commerce, or allured by the natural attractions of the country, exerted the ſame ſpirit in cultivation he did in trade, and, by ſecuring his riches in the ſoil, rendered their benefits permanent to future generations. The princes of Flanders afforded peculiar encouragement to theſe exertions, and judiciouſly beſtowed premiums on thoſe who excelled in the moſt uſeful of all occupations. The effects of ſo fortunate a combination of circumſtances ſoon became viſible. As early as the twelfth century, the foreſts of Flanders were extirpated; canals were formed, which at once drained the country, and opened a communication between its moſt diſtant diſtricts. The Scheld, reſtrained to its proper bed by the neceſſary precautions, no longer deſolated the country it ſhould enrich; the ſoil was laid open to the beneficial influence of the atmoſphere; and Flanders became the moſt fertile and cultivated portion of Europe.

A variety of well-known caufes, not here neceffary to be enumerated, have deprived thofe countries of the commerce which they once poffeffed; their agriculture, however, feels no decay, and ftill affords employment to the numerous inhabitants. The manufactures of Louvain have difappeared; the trade of Antwerp is extinct; and many of its other cities have been depopulated; but the fields of Flanders retain their fertility; their population is augmented almoft beyond parallel, and they afford an irrefragable proof, that agriculture is the moft folid bafis of national profperity. Even the ravages of war are not able to deprive agriculture of the firm poffeffion of the foil which it once obtains. In the fixteenth century, a period the moft unprofperous to thefe provinces, when all their other arts declined or difappeared, the cultivation of the earth retained its native vigour: during the almoft continued tranquillity of the prefent, it has progreffively advanced to ftill higher improvement. Their hufbandry (if not injured by late commotions) is now unequalled in any part of Europe; their population furpaffed by none; their inhabitants feel no want of employment; and their comfortable habitations, wholefome food, and the decent competence they enjoy, exprefs, in ftrongeft terms, to the delighted traveller, that each fhares the plenty which pervades his fields.

The prefent ftate of Lombardy and Tufcany would lead us to fimilar conclufions. Though the misfortunes of Italy, in the fifteenth and fixteenth century, confiderably injured the commerce and manufactures of their cities, the furrounding country is ftill one of the moft cultivated and populous in Europe.

If any thing be wanting to prove, that agriculture is the great and fecure fource of profperity and employment to the people, and that which every government fhould principally encourage, let the opinion of the ingenious Raynal be heard: if any arguments he adduces have been anticipated, his eloquence will at leaft relieve, after the dry difcuffion of fuch political topics. "Sans la culture des terres, tout com-
" merce eft précaire; parce qu'il manque des
" premiers fonds, qui font les productions de

 " la

“ la nature. Les nations qui ne ſont que ma-
“ ritimes, ou commerçantes, ont bien les fruits
“ de commerce ; mais l'arbre en appartient aux
“ peuples agricoles. L'agriculture eſt donc la
“ premiere, et la veritable richeſſe d'un état.
“ Tout en effet depend & réſulte de la culture
“ des terres. Elle fait la force intérieure des
“ états. Elle y attire les richeſſes du dehors.
“ Toute puiſſance qui vient d'ailleurs que de
“ la terre, eſt artificielle & précaire, ſoit dans
“ le phyſique, ſoit dans le moral. L'induſtrie
“ & le commerce qui ne s'exercent pas en
“ premier lieu, ſur l'agriculture d'un pays, ſont
“ au pouvoir des nations étrangeres, qui peu-
“ vent ou les diſputer par l'émulation, ou les
“ ôter par l'envie ; ſoit en établiſſant la même
“ induſtrie chez elles, ſoit en ſupprimant l'ex-
“ portation de leurs matieres en nature, ou
“ l'importation de ces matieres en œuvre. Mais
“ un état bien défriché, bien cultivé, produit
“ les hommes par les fruits de la terre, et les
“ richeſſes par les hommes. Ce ne ſont pas les
“ dents du dragon qu'il ſeme pour enfanter les
“ ſoldats, qui ſe détruiſent, c'eſt le lait de Junon,
“ qui

" qui peuple le ciel d'une multitude innombrable " d'étoiles.

" Le gouvernement doit donc sa protection aux " campagnes plutôt qu'aux villes. Les unes " sont des mères et des nourrices toujours fé- " condes, les autres ne sont que des filles souvent " ingrates et steriles. Les villes ne peuvent " guerre subsister que du superflu de la popula- " tion, et de la reproduction de la campagne. " Les places meme, & les ports de commerce, " qui par leurs vaisseaux semblent tenir au monde " entier, qui répandent plus de richesses qu'elles " n'en possedent, n'attirent cependant tous les " trésors qu'elles versent, qu'avec les produc- " tions des campagnes qui les environnent. " C'est donc à la racine qu'il faut arroser l'ar- " bre. Les villes ne seront florissantes, que par " la fécondité des champs. L'intérêt du gouverne- " ment est dont de favoriser les cultivateurs, " avant toutes les classes oiseuses de la société. " Les cultivateurs méritent la préférence du gou- " vernement, même sur les manufactures, & les " arts, soit méchaniques, soit libéraux. Ho-

" norer

" norer et protéger les arts de luxe, ſans ſonger
" aux campagnes, ſource de l'induſtrie qui les
" a crées, & les ſoutient, c'eſt oublier l'ordre
" des rapports de la nature, & de la ſociété. Fa-
" voriſer les arts, et négliger l'agriculture, c'eſt
" ôter les pierres des fondemens d'une pyramide,
" pour élever le ſommet."

Let it not be imagined, from what has been advanced, that it is our opinion manufactures ſhould be diſcouraged. On the contrary, it is evident that a number of manufacturers afford many and conſiderable encouragements to agriculture, and uſeful employment to many of the people. They raiſe a near and ready market for the ſurplus produce of the huſbandman's labour. They ſtimulate him to induſtry and employment, by preſenting various articles of convenience or ornament to his purchaſe; and the capital acquired by them is often ultimately laid out in the cultivation of the earth. " Toute nation
" agricole," ſays Raynal, " doit avoir des arts
" pour employer ſes matieres, & doit augmen-
" ter ſes productions, pour entretenir ſes arti-
" ſans.

" ſans. Si elle ne connoiſſoit que les travaux " de la terre, ſon induſtrie ſeroit bornée dans " ſes cauſes, ſes moyens, & ſes effets. Avec " peu de deſirs & de beſoins, elle feroit peu " d'efforts, elle employeroit moins de bras, & " travailleroit moins de tems. Elle ne ſauroit " accroître ni perfectionner la culture. Si cette " nation avoit à proportion plus d'arts que de " matiere, elle tomberoit à la merci des étran- " gers, qui mineroit ſes manufactures, en faiſant " baiſſer le prix de ſon luxe, et monter le prix " de ſa ſubſiſtance. Mais quand un peuple " agricole réunit l'induſtrie à la proprieté, la " culture des productions, à l'art de les em- " ployer, il a dans lui-même toutes les fa- " cultés de ſon exiſtence, & de ſa conſerva- " tion, tous les germes de ſa grandeur & de " ſa proſperité. C'eſt à ce peuple qu'il eſt " donné, de pouvoir tout ce qu'il veut, & de " vouloir tout ce qu'il peut."

Manufactures ſhould, on theſe and many other accounts, ever claim peculiar attention from the legiſlature, and ſhould meet with every aſſiſt-

ance

ance consistent with the interests of those members of the community not engaged in them, and who always form the majority of a great nation.

The positions we wish to establish are, that of all the different branches of labour, agriculture is that which affords the most productive, secure, and extensive employment to the people. That commerce and manufactures should be considered as subservient to its interests, and that they should not be encouraged at the expence and to the detriment of those engaged in its pursuits. Let us conclude, therefore, in the words of Doctor Campbell, that in these islands, as well as in every other country of similar nature and extent, "agriculture and "manufactures are twins, and must always wax "or wane with each other. It ought, there-"fore be the object both of the landed and "trading interests, to encourage agriculture, "taken in the most extensive sense, as the "mother and support of arts, as the great and "permanent principle of our domestic policy, "on

“ on which our attention muſt be invariably. “ fixed, if we mean to preſerve that felicity, “ to which the beneficence of Providence has “ given us an inconteſtible, and, if we are “ not wanting to ourſelves, an indefeaſible “ title.”

PART II.

Objects to be considered in this division of the Essay —Conclusions must be still rather general than particular, and why—A political survey of the kingdom recommended—Division of the subject.

IN this division of our Essay, our views are to be concentrated on the situation and productions of one nation; the general character, habits, and propensities, of its inhabitants; their political situation, both with respect to internal government, and external connection; their progress in agriculture, arts, and manufactures; and the possibility and means of improving, encouraging and extending them. These, and many other

other circumſtances, are immediately or remotely connected with the ſubject; and muſt be either briefly diſcuſſed, or intimately conſidered, if we be deſirous to diſcover the beſt means of providing employment for the inhabitants in general of this our iſland. In forming opinions upon theſe points, we ſhall receive no inconſiderable aſſiſtance from thoſe generally applicable obſervations and maxims, advanced in the foregoing diviſion; and it is hoped that the preceding diſcuſſion of them will not only afford the expected aid in the enſuing portion of our labours, but that the *general* concluſions deduced in the antecedent pages will receive further confirmation from thoſe of a more particular nature, which we ſhall hereafter endeavour to eſtabliſh.

Notwithſtanding, however, our views muſt at preſent be naturally more confined, our obſervations more appropriate, than heretofore; yet, any concluſions we can form with reſpect to the beſt mode of providing employment for the people of our iſland, muſt be ſtill conſidered rather as general than particular. The diverſity of habits, character, and productions, even in the ſame nation, are

are ſuch, that they muſt, as has before been noticed, occaſion a diverſity in its different diſtricts, as to the beſt mode of providing employment for their ſeveral inhabitants. The diſcovery of the nature of ſuch diverſities, however, and of the beſt mode of accommodating themſelves to, or taking advantage of their reſpective ſituations, may in this, as in ſeveral other inſtances, be in a great meaſure truſted to the individuals more immediately concerned. Their local knowledge naturally renders them the beſt judges in theſe caſes; ſelf-intereſt will neceſſarily prompt them to purſue the beſt modes of bettering their circumſtances, increaſing their capital, and conſequently of promoting the employment of the people; and in the promotion of private intereſt, inevitably improves that of ſociety at large.

A more intimate acquaintance, indeed, with the advantages and diſadvantages of the different diviſions of the iſland, and of the ſources of employment which ſhould conſequently be preferred in each, would undoubtedly be promoted by a more accurate local examination of them, than has

yet

yet been carried into execution. A political ſurvey of this nature affords ample room for a very uſeful and intereſting performance; and its encouragement would confer additional praiſe on the Academy, which has propoſed the preſent ſubject of diſcuſſion. The Author of this Eſſay, however, is perfectly inadequate to the taſk, nor is he ſingular, moſt probably, in ſuch deficiency. A ſurvey of this nature would be beſt conducted by perſons properly qualified, reſident in each county; and conſequently either already beſt informed as to their circumſtances and productions, or beſt calculated, from ſituation and connection, to acquire ſuch information. Our obſervations, therefore, will be rather applicable to the kingdom at large, than to its ſeparate diviſions; and if ſuch general concluſions as we ſhall attempt to eſtabliſh be founded in truth, the particular management of the diverſity of intereſts alluded to may be truſted to the ſpeculations of individuals, and the progreſs of that capital and knowledge which are daily increaſing throughout the kingdom.

Any facts, obſervations, and reaſonings, either remotely applicable to, or immediately connected with, the inveſtigation of the beſt means of providing employment for the people of Ireland, appear eaſily referrable to the following heads, into which we ſhall accordingly diſtribute the ſubject.

We ſhall,

I. Take a brief review of the ſituation, general productions, and climate of our iſland.

II. We ſhall conſider the general character, habits, and propenſities of the people which inhabit it. And,

III. We ſhall endeavour to determine the beſt mode of providing them with employment, under the ſeparate heads of, 1. Agriculture. 2. Manufacture. And, 3. Commerce.

SECTION I.

Of the Situation, general Productions, and Climate of Ireland.

Situation of Ireland—Productions—Fertility and diverſity of ſoil · Climate—Natural advantages on the whole conſiderable.

THE diſcuſſion of the ſubject of the preſent ſection ſhall be brief and conciſe. What our ſeveral advantages are, is in general ſufficiently underſtood; the diſcovery of the beſt means of employing, and availing ourſelves of them, is more the ſubject and aim of the preſent Eſſay, than a particular detail and minute enumeration of each.

The ſituation of Ireland is peculiarly favourable to the promotion of employment, and encouragement of induſtry. Placed, as it were, between the New and Old World, poſſeſſing an

eaſy

eaſy communication with the ports of the former, and contiguous to the ſhores of the richeſt diſtricts of the latter, it would ſeem deſtined by nature to enjoy a conſiderable portion of that commerce and intercourſe between both, which has been the ſource of riches, employment and induſtry to ſo many nations. The local circumſtances of an inſular ſtate, commodious havens, and numerous rivers, navigable, or eaſily rendered ſuch, combine with the advantages of its relative ſituation, to afford its inhabitants every encouragement and aſſiſtance in commercial purſuits, which in theſe reſpects can be expected from nature.

The utility of its natural productions and fertility of its ſoil, are equally pregnant with favourable opportunities for the exertion of induſtry, and the employment of the natives of the iſland. Of the firſt, a ſtronger proof cannot be given than that her natural productions are almoſt perfectly ſimilar to thoſe of Great Britain; a country in which both induſtry and employment flouriſh as conſiderably as in any ancient or modern nation of Europe. And as to natural fertility, ſufficient teſtimony is borne to the advantages of our iſland in this reſpect by Mr. Young. "There are people," ſays he, "who will ſmile when they hear that, in pro-"portion to the ſize of the two countries, Ire-"land is more cultivated than England; hav-"ing much leſs waſte land of all ſorts.—Natu-"ral fertility, acre for acre, over the two king-"doms, is certainly in favour of Ireland." With reſpect to ſoil, Ireland poſſeſſes another great advantage, in enjoying a conſiderable diverſity thereof: by far the greateſt portion of her ſurface is calculated for every operation and production of tillage; vaſt tracts, however, of rocky and mountainous ground are beſt adapted for breeding and rearing black cattle, which are expeditiouſly fattened on the moiſt and low ſituated plains, which could not be with equal advantage ſubmitted to the culture of the huſbandman. On many other extenſive diſtricts, the ſoil is ſo light and thin, the rock ſo near the ſurface, and ſmaller ſtones ſo abundant, that any attempt at reducing them to tillage muſt prove fruitleſs. On ſuch, however, eſpecially if the rock be limeſtone, numerous herds of ſheep

are

are not only reared, but fattened. I have ſeen large ſheep, fat enough for the table, on ground where the thinly ſcattered herbage merely ſprouted through the crevices of the rock, and where the traveller would be apt to imagine their very ſubſiſtence muſt be difficult and precarious.

As another great advantage in our ſoil may be mentioned the very great abundance of calcareous manures, as ſea-ſand, marle, but more particularly limeſtone, which, from the vicinity of either coal, culm, or turf, may be burned at a comparatively trifling expence.

With reſpect to climate, Ireland, though poſſeſſed of the principal advantages naturally attendant on her ſituation in the temperate Zone, is ſubject to one inconvenience, from her vicinity to the great Atlantic. I mean a conſiderable degree of moiſture in the atmoſphere. The weſterly winds, which ſo generally prevail, waft hither the humidity and vapours, elevated from ſo great an expanſe of ocean: broken by our mountains, or deſcending from the more unknown cauſes which occaſion the immediate fall of rain, the clouds frequently deluge the country, and prove injurious, eſpecially in harveſt time, to the different productions of the earth, particularly to every ſpecies of corn. This has been proved by regiſtries of the weather, kept in different parts of the iſland, and compared with others in different countries. This circumſtance appears, however, not to have been examined with a ſufficient degree of attention; the author of this Eſſay is at preſent engaged in an attempt to aſcertain the difference more preciſely than has yet been done. In eſtimating the degree of moiſture in a climate, we are to take into account not only the quantity of rain which falls, but the leſs perceptible humidity of the atmoſphere. The hygrometer would probably ſhew, that this is conſiderable in Ireland; the experiment, however, remains to be tried; the ſuppoſition hitherto reſts upon vague conjecture, or inconcluſive facts.

The humidity of the climate of Ireland, which is certainly favourable to the growth of herbage, has been adduced as an agument why its inhabitants ſhould turn their attention principally to paſturage,

pasturage, in preference to tillage; the injuries, however, which it occasions to the culture of corn, are more inconsiderable than is generally imagined: little is, I believe, upon the whole, lost by what is called *lodging* from rain; and as to saving, the efficacy of a few dry days is all that is necessary, which are rarely wanting, except, perhaps, in such seasons as the last, when rain prevailed so universally all over Europe. The late advances of the Irish, in the culture of corn, are sufficient to shew, that fears on this head are in a great measure groundless: and from another consideration, the unusual proportion of rain, which falls in Ireland in the earlier months, will be found not only useful, but in some measure necessary, to its agriculture: the circumstance alluded to is the general natural dryness and rockiness of the soil, which has been well noticed by Mr. Young, and which requires a greater proportion of moisture, than the deeper, heavier, and more humid clays of England. "The circumstance," says he, "which strikes me, as the greatest singularity of Ireland, is the rockiness of the soil. "Stone is so general, that I have reason to be-

"lieve

“ lieve the whole iſland is one vaſt rock of
“ different ſtrata and kinds, riſing out of the
“ ſea—in general it appears on the ſurface in
“ every part of the kingdom; the flatteſt and
“ moſt fertile parts, as Limerick, Tipperary and
“ Meath, have it at no great depth, almoſt as
“ much as the more barren ones.”

On the whole we may conclude, that the inhabitants of our iſland have little or nothing with which they can reproach nature; that her ſituation, ſoil, productions, and climate, are ſuch as afford the ampleſt ſcope for the exertion and employment of the induſtrious; and that if her ſons are deficient in either, the cauſes are to be ſought for, not in natural diſadvantages, which do not exiſt, but in ſome political defects, which ſhould be examined, developed, and corrected.

SECTION II.

Of the general Character, Habits, and Propensities of the People of Ireland.

Knowledge of the character of a people a necessary preliminary—Human nature ultimately the same, and character formed by political causes only—Supposition of natural inferiority more prevalent than is generally imagined—Climate has little effect in the formation of character—Plenty of food supposed to render the Irish indolent—This idea refuted—Conclusion to be formed on this subject—Principal objects to be held in view in this inquiry—Irish divided into three classes—Middle rank, who composed of—Their general characteristics impede national industry and employment, and how—Bucks, who composed of, and how conducted—Folly of the propensity to educate children to gentlemanly professions—Character of the inferior class of Irish—Their idleness—Thievery—Cunning and lying—Flattery—Drunkenness—Riotousness—Propensity to combinations,

tions, and breach of the laws—All tend to obstruct industry and employment—Character daily improving—Political causes of the character of the middle rank—Character of their original ancestors—Power of such character in forming that of posterity—Restraints on industrious pursuits another cause—Characteristics of the lower class may be traced to political causes, particularly oppression and poverty—Historical view of the oppression of the lower Irish, by their own chiefs—Instances of this—The English aggravated their miseries—Proofs—Some little improvement in the reign of James I. *but of short duration—Lower Irish of even the present day exposed to oppression—Proofs of this—Poverty of the lower Irish—To these causes is the present character of the lower Irish to be traced—Effects of oppression on the character, in producing idleness, flattery, cunning and lying, and a lawless spirit—Union of oppression and poverty produces thieving, ebriety, and combinations—Amendment of character to be effected by removing the causes we have noticed, and by a proper system of education.*

SECTION II.

IN determining the beſt means of promoting the induſtry and employment of a people, or of introducing any political improvement whatever among them, the diſcuſſion and inveſtigation of their real general character appears an abſolutely neceſſary preliminary. Such an inquiry will not only aſſiſt in diſcovering the moſt ſucceſsful means of effecting the deſired improvements, but as the general character of a people ſeems to be almoſt entirely regulated by moral and political cauſes, it will lead to the true ſource of thoſe obſtructions to any endeavours of this nature, which muſt naturally be encountered.

That the human race is ultimately the ſame in all ſituations; that there exiſts no innate or natural incapability in any diviſion of our ſpecies; and that the character of man is formed and modified by moral and political cauſes almoſt entirely, are poſitions which are very generally

nerally admitted, and, if this were the place for ſuch diſcuſſions, might be here eaſily demonſtrated. Intereſt, ignorance, and a ſuperficial philoſophy, indeed, have ſeverally countenanced an oppoſite opinion. The remorſeleſs Spaniard, on invading America, with confidence pronounced its natives were a race of beings diſtinct from, and inferior to, Europeans: a philoſopher has been found, to give the ſemblance of rational ſupport to the idea *, and a Biſhop has been ſeen pleading the ſame cauſe, in ſolemn council, before his ſovereign, and attempting to prove, that the miſerable ſavages on whom his countrymen had laid the talons of cruelty and rapacity, were incapable of civilization, and *naturally* deſtined for ſervitude. Similar are the aſſertions of the planter reſpecting the negro who groans beneath his laſh; nor has the defence of ſuch aſſertions been unattempted by the pen of vain and ſelf-ſufficient preſumption, or of ſtill more culpable venality.

If

* M. Pau Recherches Philoſophiques ſur les Americains.

If we descend to the more familiar relations of comparative riches and knowledge, or difference of situation; it will be found, on close inspection, that this idea of natural inferiority is not completely abandoned. Who has not heard it asserted by the haughty favourite of fortune, or the distinguished by hereditary rank, that the lower class were *naturally* stupid, vicious, and incorrigible? Who has not heard it advanced as a maxim, that the mere Irish were a peculiar people, *naturally* averse to industry, and incapable of civilization? I have more than once known the supercilious and superficial possessor of extensive estates, adduce in proof of this idea, his own conduct and experience. He, forsooth, bestowed on some the luxury of glass windows, which were speedily demolished and never renewed; he erected for others of his tenantry clean and comfortable habitations, which were soon converted into receptacles of dirt. But, to account for the first circumstance, he need only have recollected, that his tenant had not, perhaps, wherewithal to repair those accidents to which glass, especially in such habitations, is liable; and that, in the second, a sudden

den change of circumſtances could never have altered or eradicated general and inveterate *habits*, engendered in a ſtate of barbarity, increaſed by oppreſſion, and perſiſted in from poverty. If the deſcendants of his remote and barbarous anceſtor, whether a Saxon Baron, or a Mileſian Chief, had been continually expoſed to the operation of ſimilar cauſes, their improvement would have been as trifling, and his taſte for cleanlineſs and the artificial neceſſaries of life as faint, as that of the vaſſal he affects to accuſe of natural inferiority †.

The difference of climate has by many writers been ſuppoſed conſiderably to influence the human

† The dirt of the Engliſh, at preſent a very clean nation, was at a late period remarkable. Eraſmus complains of their extreme ſlovenlineſs and uncleanlineſs, and attributes to it the frequent plagues with which they were infeſted: he viſited England in the reign of Henry VIII. "Their floors," ſays he, "are commonly "ſtrewed with ruſhes, under which lies unmoleſted a "collection of beer, greaſe, fragments, bones, ſpittle, "excrements of dogs and cats, and every thing that is "nauſeous." Epiſt. 432.

So late as Elizabeth's reign thoſe ſaid ſtraw floors were very common, even in the palace.

man mind, and confequently to alter the capabilities and propenfities of man, in various regions of the globe. I am very ftrongly inclined to imagine, that this doctrine has been extended confiderably beyond its juft limits; and that the power of climate in this refpect is indeed trifiing. Any difcuffion of the fubject, however, would be at prefent inapplicable; the fituation of our ifland, in the temperate region of the temperate Zone, where, even according to the theory alluded to, the mental faculties are moft perfect, precludes any fuppofition of the qualities of its natives being from *climate* inferior to thofe of other nations, or in nature peculiar to themfelves.

But another national caufe of barbarity, indolence, and defect of civilization, has been difcovered. The Irifh, living principally upon a root, which, cultivated with little trouble, affords a confiderable abundance of food, can therefore never become induftrious, refined, or civilized. This idea appears to have been firft ftarted by Sir William Temple. "In Ireland," fays he, "by the largenefs and plenty of food, and fcar- "city of people, all things neceffary to life are

"fo

" ſo cheap, that an induſtrious man by two " days labour may gain enough to feed him " the reſt of the week; which I take to be a " very plain ground for the lazineſs attributed " to the people." *Obſervations on the United Provinces*, p. 120. A ſimilar ſentiment has been adopted by Hume, and inſiſted on by Sir John Dalrymple and others. Were the Iriſh in a ſtate of perfect barbarity, and acquainted with no other incentive to labour than the mere appetite for food, this ſentiment, as has been obſerved in the firſt part, might have ſome weight; but, in the period of civilization they have for ſome time arrived at, the abundance of food, which neceſſarily reſults from the culture of the uſeful plant in queſtion, the potatoe, inſtead of retarding, muſt promote the increaſe of capital, the conſequent induſtry and employment, and the ultimate civilization of the people. This will be ſufficiently evident from the general conſiderations advanced in the diviſion of this Eſſay already referred to; as an additional proof, take the opinion of Doctor Smith: " If in any " country the common and favourite vegetable " food of the people ſhould be drawn from a

" plant,

" plant, of which the moſt common land, with " the ſame culture, produced a much greater " quantity than the moſt fertile does of corn; the " rent of the landlord would neceſſarily be much " greater; and ſhould potatoes become in any " part of Europe, like rice in ſome rice coun- " tries, the common and favourite vegetable " food of the people, the ſame quantity of cul- " tivated land would maintain a much greater " number of people, and the labourers being " generally fed with potatoes, a greater ſurplus " would remain, after replacing all the ſtock, " and maintaining all the labour employed in " cultivation." Mr. Young's opinion of the queſtion is as follows: " Is it, or is it not, a " matter of conſequence, for the great body of " the people of a country, to ſubſiſt upon that " ſpecies of food which is produced in the " greateſt quantity by the ſmalleſt ſpace of land? " One need only *ſtate*, in order to *anſwer*, the " queſtion. It certainly is an object of the " higheſt conſequence."

Leaving, therefore, all preſumptions or intereſted aſſertions, all mean and illiberal prejudices, reſpecting

respecting the natural incapacity, or inherent and incorrigible vices, of nations or of ranks, to the further refutation of those writers who have already successfully undertaken it, or to that resulting from their own intrinsic and apparent obscurity; let the philanthropic mind view with pity, not condemnation, any deficiencies, vices or miseries, which distress a people. Let them be traced to their true source and origin, political errors and mistakes: let these be particularly investigated, and if possible corrected or removed. So shall the capabilities of improvement which all ranks and descriptions of men possess be gradually expanded and unfolded; their industry, employment, and happiness, feel proportionate increase; and the favours of fortune, and advantages of superior information, prompt those who are possessed of such blessings, to alleviate the inconveniencies of nations and of ranks, by prudent and applicable assistance, not to aggravate their distresses by supercilious reproach and unmerited calumny.

In investigating the character of the Irish nation, our principal aim shall be to discover what are the predominant defects, which may check and obstruct the employment of its people. On examination it will be found, that the principal deformities which pollute it are precisely of this nature. In tracing the portrait, though we shall avoid caricature on the one hand, we shall equally disdain flattery on the other. The delineation of the natural lines shall be our principal aim. National partiality might prompt us to soften the harsher features, and throw into relief the more favourable ; but such conduct would be that of the patient, who conceals from his physician the symptoms of the disease for which his assistance is required. If deficiencies in national character arise, as we have asserted, from political errors, the more generally they are known the more probable becomes the chance of their removal. We shall, therefore, sketch them, as far as in us lies, with a bold yet faithful hand. We shall investigate when possible the causes from which they have originated ; and notice the most efficacious and applicable remedies which can be employed for their correction or removal.

The people of Ireland may be divided into three claſſes; the high, the middle, and the commonalty. The firſt there is no neceſſity of noticing; they differ little from their neighbours in England, and their vices or virtues can but ſlightly affect the employment of the other inferior ranks of community.

By the middle rank of Iriſhmen, I do not underſtand a wealthy and reſpectable yeomanry. So valuable a diviſion of citizens we are yet, alas! unacquainted with. Neither do I, in this claſs, include the mercantile part of the community, although they properly belong thereto.—They do not, it is true, poſſeſs the ſpirit of induſtry, and application to buſineſs, which thoſe of the ſame deſcription do in England and Holland; but they are not ſo addicted to diſſipation and extravagance as the middle rank of country gentlemen. They hold, it may be ſaid, an intermediate rank with reſpect to induſtry; poſſeſſing neither the ſcrupulouſly attentive ſpirit of buſineſs and induſtry, which diſtinguiſhes the Engliſh merchant, nor the unthinking ſpirit of extravagance which ruins the Iriſh *gentleman*.

The

The claſs I ſpeak of is principally compoſed of men of ſmall eſtates, who generally live beyond their income; and thoſe landholders known by the name of *middle-men*, who take large diſtricts of the country from thoſe poſſeſſed of extenſive eſtates, and either cover them with black cattle and ſheep, or re-let them at extravagant rents to wretched and indigent cottagers. The injuries this deſcription of people occaſion to the agriculture of the kingdom we ſhall hereafter have occaſion to explain; their character, ſo far as reſpects the induſtry and employment of the people, is here only to be examined. Let me premiſe, that I ſhall delineate in this, as in every other inſtance, merely a *general* one; many exceptions to it exiſt, and I am happy to ſee ſuch are daily increaſing. Still, however, it will be found the predominant character, and one which muſt conſiderably obſtruct the general employment and induſtry of any ſociety wherein it prevails.

The general characteriſtics of the claſs of ſociety I ſpeak of, are diſſipation, idleneſs, and vanity. Every man with a few acres of land,

and a moderate revenue, is dignified, as a matter of courſe, with the title of *Eſquire;* and, be his family ever ſo numerous, the incumbrances on his little patrimony ever ſo conſiderable, he muſt ſupport a pack of hounds, entertain with claret, or if not able, with whiſkey; keep a chaiſe and livery ſervants, and ape, in ſhort, his ſuperiors in every reſpect. Meanwhile his debts are increaſing, his creditors growing clamorous, and every induſtrious occupation, which might relieve his diſtreſſes, neglected, as utterly beneath the dignity of a *gentleman.*

The numerous inſtances of this nature which occur cannot but poſſeſs a very ſerious, extenſive, and powerful influence in the obſtruction and depreſſion of national induſtry and employment. The bad debts of men of buſineſs are more numerous in Ireland than can well be imagined: ſuch muſt conſiderably injure and obſtruct the induſtrious. Thoſe ſums which ſhould be ſaved for the younger children of the family, and laid out in the eſtabliſhment of ſome induſtrious occupation, that would enable them to afford employment to thouſands of their countrymen,

are

are either ſquandered in idle extravagance, or, if collected from the fortune which the hopeful heir apparent may obtain in matrimony, are employed by thoſe on whom they are beſtowed, in purſuing the laudable example they have been accuſtomed to from infancy. But the influence of ſuch example is ſtill more extenſive: its ruinous contagion extends to the moſt inferior ranks. The labouring hind quits his ſpade, to purſue his landlord's pack of beagles on foot, and at night intoxicates himſelf with whiſkey, while his maſter enjoys a ſimilar pleaſure with liquors more refined and palatable.

To the ſame ſource are we to trace thoſe nuiſances to every rank of ſociety, denominated *bucks* and *buckeens*. Such, in general, are either the eldeſt ſons of the gentlemen of ſmall property we have deſcribed; or the younger children of thoſe poſſeſſed of larger, who have received their ſcanty pittance, of which the augmentation by induſtrious means is never once attempted, and the final diſſipation, one would imagine, deemed impoſſible. To ſtand behind a counter, ſuperintend a farm, or calculate in a compting-

compting-houſe, would be beneath the dignity of ſuch exalted beings, and diſgrace the memory of their *gentlemen* anceſtors. But would not ſuch purſuits be finally more uſeful to their country, and more grateful to their own feelings, than a mode of life which diſſipates the funds that ſhould be employed in induſtry, corrupts the manners of the people, ruins the health and annihilates the fortune of the individual, and, in general, finally leads them to ſubſiſt as mendicants on the charity of ſome more opulent relation. 'Tis diſguſting to ſee ſuch beings gaming at a hazard table, buſtling at a horſe race, quarrelling over their claret, or hallooing after a fox, arrayed, perhaps, in an equipage they have neither inclination nor ability to pay for. Let us turn from the picture—the only ſatisfaction attendant on its examination is, that the ſpecies are daily diminiſhing. May they ſpeedily be extinct.

To the ſame general averſion to induſtry, and tendency to diſſipation, and to a conſiderable ſhare of family vanity, are we to aſcribe the ſilly, but more excuſable, propenſity of *gentlemen*, to to educate their children in *gentlemanly* profeſſions. Hence ariſe the daily increaſing numbers of curates with ſcanty ſalaries, or none, attornies preying on the public, enſigns without the means of riſing higher, phyſicians without patients, and lawyers without briefs. More advantageous would it be, as well to the individuals immediately concerned, as to the general employment of the people, if they had been bred to induſtrious occupations, wherein ſucceſs, with prudence, is almoſt certain; and wherein the capital expended in their education would be laid out with greater advantage to themſelves, and the inevitable increaſe of employment to the people.

The character of the inferior claſs of the community comes next to be conſidered; and, as more intimately connected with the queſtion reſpecting the beſt means of providing employment for the people, demands attentive examination. I ſhall, as in the preceding inſtance, chiefly conſider thoſe traits which have obvious reference to the ſubject before us.

Two leading and naturally allied features in the character of the lower Irish, as connected with this subject, are idleness and inquisitiveness, especially when hired and employed to perform the work of others. The prevalence of these principles must be obvious to any person who has in the remotest degree been conversant in country affairs, or who ever, as a traveller, has cast an observant glance on the conduct of the labouring peasantry. The moment an overseer quits them they inevitably drop their work, take snuff, and fall into chat as to the news of the day: no traveller can pass them without diverting their attention from the business in hand, and giving rise to numerous surmises as to his person, errand, and destination. The most trivial occurrence, especially in the sporting line, will hurry them, unless restrained, from their occupations. Even the sedentary manufacturer will, on such occasions, quit his employment. Nothing is more common than to see a weaver in the North start from his loom on hearing a pack of hounds, and pursue them through a long and fatiguing chase.

A tendency

A tendency to pilfering and theft is very predominant among the lower claſſes of the Iriſh. To any perſon acquainted with them this requires no proof; and it is highly detrimental to thoſe poſſeſſed of capital, who wiſh to enter into the extenſive practice of any branch of induſtry among them, but eſpecially of agriculture. I have known twenty ſheaves of corn reckoned into each ſtack at night, in a very extenſive field, and one out of each was miſſing next morning. Of this tendency many ſimilar inſtances might be given. Let one ſuffice.

Connected with this vice is the prevalence of a low cunning, and of lying, which is very obſervable among them; and, as their accompaniment, may be mentioned a fawning flattery. The blunt honeſty, the bold independence of the Engliſh yeoman, are wanting; and in their place too generally ſubſtituted the petty diſhoneſty of the vaſſal, the ſervility and artifice of the ſlave.

Drunkenneſs is an evil of conſiderable magnitude, in the catalogue of national vices. It

is

is one to which the lower Irifh are peculiarly addicted, and that from which the moft ferious obftructions arife to their induftry and employment. That vile beverage, whifkey, fo cheaply purchafed, and fo generally diffufed, affords them an eafy opportunity of gratifying this deftructive paffion; and, where they are, from habit and example, ftrongly enough addicted to the crime, prefents them an additional temptation, by the facility with which it is obtained. I know no evil which more ftrongly demands the interference of the legiflature, or which requires more efficacious meafures to be adopted for its diminution.

As one confequence of the general prevalence of ebriety, the lower Irifh are remarkably riotous. I do not here fo much allude to Whiteboyifm, and other public difturbances, which owe their origin chiefly to other caufes, as to their quarrels among themfelves. Their fairs are frequently the fcenes of confufion, riot, difturbance and bloodfhed: fired with the fumes of whifkey, one acquaintance quarrels with another; the friends of each efpoufe his caufe, *their* relations

relations and acquaintances inevitably fall in as parties, till the quarrel ſpreading in compound progreſſion includes, perhaps, a majority of the multitude. Inſtances, indeed, of this nature are becoming every day conſiderably leſs frequent.

Combinations, riſings, and outrage, among tradeſmen, are far from unuſual. Their pretexts upon ſuch occaſions are often truly ridiculous. I have known a tumultuous mob of coopers aſſemble in one city to demoliſh the ſtores of a merchant, becauſe he found it advantageous to export ſome of his hog's fleſh ſaved as bacon, and conſequently required ſomewhat a ſmaller number of caſks than when all was exported ſaved as pork; and on five being taken up and confined, the bakers refuſed to bake, and the butchers to kill meat, till they were liberated.

Tradeſmen in Ireland have much leſs cauſe of complaint than any other claſs of labourers. Their wages are nearly as high as in England, and the natural and artificial neceſſaries of life much

much cheaper. "When it is conſidered," ſays Mr. Young, "that common labour in Ire-"land is but little more than a third of what "it is in England, it is extraordinary that ar-"tizans are paid nearly, if not full as high, as "in that kingdom."

The lower Iriſh are to a remarkable degree lawleſsly inclined. It is well known that inſtead of being anxious to apprehend offenders, or to aſſiſt the execution of the law, they are in general ready to give the former every aſſiſtance to eſcape; and to reſiſt the latter, unleſs awed by ſuperior force. Of theſe propenſities many proofs may be given, by inſtances of reſcue, forcible poſſeſſion, and other ſimilar proceedings; but the fact is too notorious to require any evidence.

Such are the predominant qualities of the Iriſh people connected with our preſent ſubject; and they all evidently tend to the diſcouragement of induſtrious purſuits, and the obſtruction of employment. The general character of the nation we are not to appreciate: innumerable good qualities

qualities might be adduced, to counterbalance the defects we have ſtated; but they partake more of the energy of courage, the warmth of patriotiſm, and generoſity of hoſpitality, than the cool, conſiderate, and prudent perſeverance of induſtry.

But however uninviting, nay diſcouraging, to the votary of this latter quality, is the picture we have drawn; one cheering conſideration reſults from the view; and that is, that the defects which have been noticed are daily diminiſhing. The middling ranks are becoming more attentive to their debts, and leſs indulgent to their extravagance. A ſpirit of induſtry is infuſing its regenerating vigour among them; the vain and ridiculous averſion to the purſuits of commerce, or other induſtrious occupations, is wearing out, and the encouragement of agriculture more generally attended to. The lower claſs are becoming more induſtrious, more wealthy, more independent: and the conſequence is, that all the ſubordinate vices we have mentioned are every day leſs frequent. In my own memory, a conſiderable amelioration in this reſpect has

has taken place. Still, however, the vices alluded to, though diminiſhing, do exiſt. We have aſſerted that all ſuch muſt be owing to political errors. Let us try and diſcover to what they are to be attributed, and enforce the neceſſity, and deviſe the means, of removing the cauſes productive of ſuch ruinous conſequences.

To determine the political ſources to which are to be traced the general diſſipation, extravagance, and want of induſtry we have deſcribed, as ſo prevalent among the middle claſs of the Iriſh, is a taſk not ſo eaſily accompliſhed, as we ſhall find a ſimilar attempt reſpecting the lower orders of the people. The general cauſes, however, may be diſcovered, and from theſe more ſubordinate ones have originated.

One fruitful ſource of the appearances deſcribed, is the general character of the anceſtors of the preſent race. Soldiers of fortune, and unacquainted with induſtrious purſuits, their ſettlement and poſſeſſions here, were obtained, not by the gradual operation of induſtry, but

the

the more rapid exertions of power. The quick ſucceſſion of revolutions and rebellions, which the iſland experienced, gave frequent occaſion to the exertions of ſuch authority, both in favour of its natives and thoſe foreigners who eſpouſed the conquering cauſe ; and confiſcation is the tenure to which by far the greater portion of the landed property of the nation may be ultimately traced. Unlike thoſe original emigrants to the northern ſtates of America, who, flying from the hand of perſecution, carried with them the habits of induſtry, they have tranſmitted to their poſterity, thoſe who were inſtantaneouſly inveſted with poſſeſſions in this iſland, without looking to futurity, ſought only to extract the moſt immediate emolument, and greateſt degree of power from their ſudden acquiſitions, and to enjoy both in the indulgence of that authority and idleneſs, hoſpitality and diſſipation, to which, from former habits, they were naturally addicted. Such is the general influence of family example, that original characters of this nature are more difficult to be eradicated, and give a tinge to ſucceeding generations for a greater length of time than can well be imagined. America affords

fords a convincing proof of the truth of this remark. The obſervant eye can diſcover, not only the obvious difference of character between the prodigal and idle Creole of Mexico, and the frugal and induſtrious planter of Connecticut, but alſo the leſs perceptible diverſity of manners which exiſts among the different tribes who inhabit the northern ſtates; and, in the firſt, as well as the latter inſtance, the judicious and hiſtoric mind may trace the ſeveral diſtinguiſhing traits of each to the peculiar characteriſtics of their original anceſtors.

Another general ſource of the idleneſs and diſſipation ſo prevalent among the middle ranks of life in Ireland, is the diſcouragement to induſtrious occupations, occaſioned by the various reſtraints under which ſhe laboured for a ſeries of years. A people, ſuch as I have deſcribed, would have required the foſtering hand of encouragement to tempt them to induſtrious undertakings; the agriculture and commerce of the iſland ſhould have been aſſiſted, at leaſt not depreſſed, and the advantages reſulting from engaging in them rendered ſo obvious, as to al-

lure

lure her natives from idleneſs and diſſipation, to the more profitable proſecution of oppoſite purſuits.

Theſe appear to have been the generally operating cauſes, to which is to be attributed that character we have deſcribed as ſo prevalent among the middle ranks of life in Ireland. Others of a ſubordinate nature may, no doubt, be diſcovered, but need not here be particularly inſiſted on, as, for the moſt part, proceeding from theſe general ſources, and not ſo much connected with the ſubject of our Eſſay.

As the prevailing characteriſtics of the middle, ſo may thoſe of the lower claſs of the inhabitants of Ireland be traced to the operation of political cauſes. The two which appear to have poſſeſſed moſt influence in the formation of their character, are Oppreſſion and Poverty. The exiſtence of theſe cauſes I ſhall firſt demonſtrate; their operation ſhall be afterwards briefly explained. Fully to comprehend the degree of oppreſſion to which the lower Iriſh have been expoſed for ages would require more particular consideration, a more minute detail, than can here be allotted to it—a general sketch must suffice, and will probably be sufficient for our purposes: and, to render it more comprehensive, we shall first take a brief historical view of their treatment for some centuries back, and afterwards consider their actual situation at present.

Whatever credit may be due to the splendid accounts of antiquarians, respecting the civilization, wise institutions, and happy state of the Irish nation in more remote ages, it is certain that at the period of the first descent of the English under Henry II. they were at any rate as barbarous and unpolished as any of the other then uncivilized states of Europe. Some writers would have us believe they were infinitely more so, but in the discussion of their comparative merits, as to this point, we are little interested. At the period alluded to, the latter end of the twelfth century, the situation of the poorer orders was all over Europe melancholy: but the Irish peasantry were at that time, and for several subsequent ages, exposed to more than ordinary

ordinary oppreſſion. The inſtitutions and cuſtoms of the country itſelf were peculiarly unfavourable to their intereſts. Their chieftains, and the heads of the ſubordinate ſepts and clans, ſeem to have poſſeſſed the power of fleecing and oppreſſing their inferiors almoſt at will; or at leaſt the pretext and rules by which their exactions were extorted were of ſuch nature, that both the liberty and property of the poor were at the mercy of every petty and deſpotic Kern.

Of this many proofs may be adduced. The inſtitution of what was termed *Coin and Livery*, originally Iriſh, and ſomething ſimilar to the inſtitution of *purveyance* in other ſtates, was as powerful an inſtrument of oppreſſion as could be entruſted to a multitude of uncivilized chiefs. This conſiſted in taking man's-meat and horſe-meat, as they were called, and money at will, from all the inhabitants of the country, for the ſupport of the ſoldiery.

The Iriſh chieftains and Taniſts exacted, as ſeignoral rights, aſſeſſments equally grievous, and ſavouring of barbarity. Such were *Coſherings*, or viſits of the lord and his family among his dependents; on whom he lived during his progreſs at free coſt. *Seſſings*, or the maintenance of his horſes and horſe-boys, dogs and dog-boys. Other exactions were practiſed under the name of *Cuttings*, *Tallages*, &c. all of which, as Sir John Davies ſays, "made the lord an "abſolute tyrant, and the tenant a very ſlave "and villain; and, in one reſpect, more mi-"ſerable than bond-ſlaves; for commonly the "bond-ſlave is fed by his lord, but here the "lord was fed by his bond-ſlave."

The deſcent of the Engliſh, inſtead of meliorating the ſituation, aggravated the miſeries of the unfortunate Iriſh peaſant. The natural progreſs of civilization might have aboliſhed thoſe oppreſſive remnants of the feodal ſyſtem, as well in Ireland as the other European ſtates. The ſettlement of the Engliſh, by throwing the kingdom into a ſtate of almoſt perpetual warfare, and conſequently protracting its civilization, not only riveted thoſe remnants of barbarity, but heaped additional miſeries on a people already devoted

devoted and oppreſſed. As barbarous and prone to oppreſſion as the chiefs they invaded, theſe ſettlers adopted, and, if I may proſtitute the expreſſion, improved on the inſtitution of coin and livery. " The Engliſh," ſays their countryman, Sir John Davies, " when they had " learned it, uſed it with more inſolence, and " made it more intolerable; for this oppreſſion " was not temporary, or limited either to place " or time; but, becauſe there was every where " a continual war, either offenſive or defenſive, " and every lord of a country and every marcher " made war and peace at his pleaſure, it be- " came univerſal and perpetual, and was, in- " deed, the moſt heavy oppreſſion that ever " was uſed in any Chriſtian or Heathen king- " dom."

The Engliſh not only oppreſſed the natives of the iſland, by adopting, and executing with increaſed rigour, the ruinous inſtitutions they found exiſting; thoſe they themſelves fabricated were equally calculated to oppreſs with additional miſeries an already wretched race. This will be ſufficiently evident from a review of the

the general conduct of the English settlers, and the inhabitants of the English pale, towards the Irish people. The latter were reputed aliens and enemies; they were allowed no compensation or remedy for any trespasses committed against them, by the inhabitants of the pale. They frequently requested to be admitted to the participation of the English laws and institutions, and were refused. Intermarriage with them was, by the statute of Kilkenny, deemed a capital crime; and their invaders had the audacity so far to insult the rights of human nature as to adjudge, that the murder of an Irishman was no felony*. How similar the sentiments entertained,

* At a general gaol delivery at Limerick, before the Lord Justice in the fourth year of Edward II. it is recorded, that "Willielmus filius Rogeri, rectatus de morte Rogeri de Canteton, felonice per ipsum "interfecti, venit & dicit, quod feloniam per interfectionem predictam committere non potuit, quia "dicit quod prædict. Rogerus *Hibernicus* est et non "de *libero sanguine*. Dicit etiam quod predict. Rogerus, "fuit de cognomine de O'Hederiscal, & non de cog- "nomine de Canteton; & de hoc ponit se super- "patriam, &c. & Jurati dicunt super sacram: suum, "quod prædict. Rogerus Hibernicus fuit, & de cog- "nomine

tertained, by their oppressors, of the West Indian negro, and Irish peasant!

From these sketches may be formed a tolerable general idea of the situation of the great mass of the Irish people from the reign of Henry II. to that of James I. Exposed to the combined insolence, extortion, and rapacity of domestic and foreign despots, the historian will scarcely be able to discover an instance in any age or country of a people more wretched and miserable, more injured and oppressed. At this period some little improvement in their situation was effected. The institution of coin and livery was abolished; the war carried on by Elizabeth had in a great measure destroyed the power of the petty chiefs throughout the kingdom; the benefits of the English law were, for the

" nomine de O'Hederiscal & pro Hibernico habebatur " tota vita sua *Ideo* prædict. Wilielmus quoad felo- " niam prædict. *quietus.* Sed quia prædict. Rogerus " O'Hederiscal fuit Hibernicus domini regis, prædictus " Wilielmus recomittatur gaolæ quousque plegios in- " venerit de *quinque Marcis solvendis* Dom. Regi pro " solutione prædicti Hibernici." *Archiv. in Castr. Dub. apud Davies.*

the firſt time, *equally* extended to all its inhabitants; and this, as Sir John Davies ſays, "though ſomewhat diſtaſteful to the Iriſh lords, "was ſweet and moſt welcome to the common people; who, albeit they were rude and "barbarous, yet did they quickly apprehend "the difference between the tyranny and oppreſſion under which they lived before, and "the juſt government and protection which we "*promiſed* unto them for the time to come."

This apparent dawn of better days was ſoon, however, to be overcaſt. The unhappy difference in religious points, which had commenced ſome years before, ripened at length to the unfortunate and infamous rebellion of 1641. This and the ſubſequent civil war in 1688, in their conſequences reduced the lower Iriſh to almoſt as wretched a ſtate as ever; and the penal code completed, under Queen Anne, a ſyſtem which pollutes the annals of the nation that gave it birth, was the concluding act of injury exerciſed over an oppreſſed, perſecuted, and at length dejected people. The liberal ſpirit of an enlightened and enlightening age has at laſt repealed

pealed the moſt obnoxious articles of this diſgraceful code. The ſituation of the peaſant has, ſince the final pacification of the kingdom, but more eſpecially ſince the ſettlement of its conſtitution in 1782, been daily improving; the exactions of a barbarous age are no longer known; but it remains to be conſidered whether the Iriſh commonalty are not ſtill expoſed to the oppreſſion of the powerful, the contumely of the rich, the inſult of the haughty.

It is equally certain, and to be lamented, that the Iriſh peaſantry of even the preſent day are expoſed to, and experience a greater degree of domeſtic tyranny than can well be imagined. A reſidence of ſome continuation among them is requiſite fully to comprehend, as well the obvious and open outrages of the unfeeling *gentleman bully*, as the various little exactions and oppreſſions of the authoritative landlord. The writer of this Eſſay has had many opportunities of knowing the real ſituation of the lower Iriſh. He might adduce inſtances from his own obſervation, of the hard treatment they frequently experience, and the extortions to which they

are

are daily expoſed: but a repetition of the former would be diſguſting, a petty detail of the latter tedious. Of both a very adequate idea may be formed from the juſt and liberal remarks of Mr. Young. We ſhall give an extract from them in place of any deſcription of our own; only remarking, that the improvement he notices has, ſince his Tour, been progreſſive, and even during ſo ſhort a period far from inconſiderable. "It muſt be very apparent to every "traveller through the country, that the la-"bouring poor are treated with harſhneſs, and "are in all reſpects ſo little conſidered, that "their want of importance ſeems a perfect con-"traſt to their ſituation in England, of which "country, comparatively ſpeaking, they reign "the ſovereigns. The age has improved ſo "much in humanity, that even the poor Iriſh "have experienced its influence; and are every "day treated better and better. But ſtill the "remnant of the old manners, the abominable "diſtinction of religion, united with the op-"preſſive conduct of the little country gentle-"men, or rather vermin of the kingdom, who "never were out of it, altogether bear ſtill

"very

" very heavy on the poor people, and ſubject " them to ſituations more mortifying than we " ever beheld in England.——A landlord in Ire- " land can ſcarcely invent an order which a ſer- " vant, labourer, or cotter, dares refuſe to exe- " cute. Nothing ſatisfies him but an unlimited " ſubmiſſion; diſreſpect, or any thing tending " towards ſaucineſs, he may puniſh with his cane " or his horſewhip with the moſt perfect ſecu- " rity. A poor man would have his bones broke " if he offered to lift his hand in his own de- " fence. Knocking down is ſpoken of in the " country in a manner that makes an Engliſh- " man ſtare.——If a poor man lodges a com- " plaint againſt a gentleman, or any animal that " chooſes to call itſelf a gentleman, and a juſ- " tice iſſues out a ſummons for his appearance, " it is a fixed affront, and he will infallibly be " *called out*. Where *manners* are in conſpiracy " againſt *law*, to whom are the oppreſſed people " to have recourſe?"—Even if an unfortunate individual, treated in the harſheſt manner, finds any Juſtice hardy enough to receive his information, and attempts to puniſh his oppreſſor at the general aſſizes, I merely aſk one ſimple queſtion—

tion—Is it not ten to one that the grand jury will throw out the bills of indictment?

The exactions and extortions which thofe faid *little* country gentlemen are guilty of, in a thoufand different ways, is too well known to require any proof; we fhall have occafion hereafter flightly to notice them.

To offer any evidence of the poverty which prevails among the Irifh commonalty would furely be fuperfluous, it is too obvious to efcape the notice of the moft inattentive, too confiderable not to poffefs a powerful influence on their character, and fo univerfally acknowledged, as to render any proof of its exiftence unneceffary. Its prevalence has probably been occafioned by the difturbed ftate of the nation for feveral ages, by the general difcouragement to induftrious purfuits already noticed, and by that oppreffion to which the peafantry have been expofed from fo many fources, and through fo many centuries.

It is not difficult to determine how the facts we have mentioned have influenced the character of the Irish commonalty, and sullied it with the defects already stated. The relation between cause and effect is probably as steady and uniform in the moral and political, as in the natural world. If the human mind be, as we suppose it, ultimately similar in every variety of our species, the same causes to whose operation it is exposed, must, in similar situations, be universally followed by similar consequences. The great difficulty in all such inquiries is, to trace the operation of the several collateral circumstances, which modify the impression of the generally operating cause.

Conformably to this leading principle, it will be found, that considerable and continued oppression has uniformly degraded the character of any unfortunate people over whom it has been exerted. In the instance before us, many of the leading traits in the character of the lower Irish may easily be traced to this original. "Extortion and oppression," as Sir John Davies says, "hath been the true cause of the "idleness of this Irish nation." Oppression is universally the parent of idleness, especially when accompanied

accompanied by exaction and rapacity; both have existed to an enormous degree among us, and both, though considerably diminished, still exist. National habits, once acquired, are not easily eradicated; and that idleness which the more open, desultory, and barbarous violence of former ages introduced, is continued by the more uniform and *gentlemanly* oppression of the present.

To the same cause are to be attributed the fawning flattery, the low cunning, the tendency to falsehood, with which our unfortunate peasantry may, with too much truth, I cannot say with too much justice, be reproached. Man resists, by nature and by instinct, the insulting arm of power; but if such resistance be unfortunately ineffectual, he seeks the debasing protection of flattery, craft, and cunning, the resources of the slave in every age and every nation. *Ingenium mala sæpe movent.* Deprived of independence, man, as well as the more inferior species of the animal creation, deserts the dignity of nature, and assumes an artificial and degrading character.

To

To the ſame oppreſſion are we to trace the lawleſs inclinations of the Iriſh peaſant. Feeling little protection from the law, he is little intereſted in its ſupport. Conſcious of the inefficacy of ſtatutes to his defence, he ſeeks the protection of his more powerful maſter*; who defends him from ſellow-lordlings, more, in general, from a ſenſe of injury which any attack on his vaſſal is ſuppoſed to convey, than from motions of philanthropy or general equity and independence. Hence, if the chief be engaged in any lawleſs attempt, if he be deſirous, for inſtance, of forcing or detaining an unwarrantable poſſeſſion, the nod is given to his dependants, and his dictates obeyed, not only without murmur, but with alacrity.

To the deſtructive influence of oppreſſion upon the character of the lower Iriſh, is added that of general and extreme poverty. To this the thieving diſpoſition they are reproached with is to be principally attributed. It is an old ſaying, that "neceſſity has no law;" and the wretch

* The common appellation for landlord in Ireland.

wretch who feels himſelf and family pinched with hunger, and expoſed in rags to the inclemency of ſeaſons, is in ſome degree excuſable in pilfering, from his oppreſſors, the means of ſcanty and temporary relief. Where the ſituation of the poor has been bettered, their thieving has been uniformly found to diminiſh: render their circumſtances comfortable, it will entirely diſappear.

The miſery and idleneſs occaſioned by poverty and oppreſſion united, is a principal ſource of the prevalent tendency to ebriety, and the conſequent riotous feuds ſo remarkable among the Iriſh. Drunkenneſs is the ſolace of miſery, the reſource of idleneſs, the great pleaſure of the uncivilized in every quarter of the world. Habit and example confirm and extend a practice ſo deſtructive; but as general wealth increaſes, and as induſtry and civilization become diffuſed, it is gradually diminiſhed, and, as a national ſtigma, at length effaced.

Combinations and outrages among tradeſmen are uſually the effects of idleneſs, drunkenneſs,

and

and poverty united. Remove the caufes, the frequency of their confequences will ceafe. Such occurrences require, befide, the immediate intervention of power: they fhould be inftantly and efficacioufly checked by the exertion of authority. An enraged rabble knows no moderation, and, ignorant of their real origin, increafe in general the evils they defire to meliorate. But while the more enlightened fhould reprefs with force fuch blind impetuofity, they fhould ufe every exertion to remove the original caufes which give it birth, nor neglect the radical, while engaged in the application of palliative remedies.

If the character we have drawn, and the fources to which it has been traced, are alike injurious to the advancement of general induftry and the employment of the people; it becomes, in the prefent Effay, an object of confiderable importance to point out the moft univerfally effectual means of altering and improving it. Such appear to be the meafures moft efficacious for removing thofe caufes, to which the general characters have been traced; and from no one, perhaps, is ſo much efficacy to be expected as from the introduction and general diffuſion of a greater degree of wealth among the lower orders of the people. Render the ſituation of the peaſant more comfortable, give him ſome little capital to enable him to proſecute his neceſſary occupations, let the defence, forbearance, or aſſiſtance of his ſuperiors be no longer neceſſary requiſites to his protection or ſubſiſtence, and he will reaſſume the dignity of independence, to which he has ſo long been a ſtranger, and ſpurn at the oppreſſion to which he now patiently ſubmits. Then would the wretch who now ſkulks behind the ſhield of ſome little deſpot, claim and feel the more equal protection of the laws, at preſent dormant, and demand as his right, what he now ſupplicates as a favour. Oppreſſion has been the principal ſource of that poverty under which he vegetates rather than lives, and the continuance of poverty prolongs this oppreſſion. The acquiſition of wealth would both enable the induſtrious to proſecute their purſuits and give additional vigour to the induſtry which ſhould animate them in the proſecution. Idleneſs and ſervility, theft and drunkenneſs, and the various ſubordinate blemiſhes mifhes of character, would difappear; and the manners of the people no longer combine, with the other misfortunes to which they have been or are expofed, to retard their induftry, and obftruct their employment †.

Another

† Let it not be for a moment imagined, that the picture we have delineated, of the former and prefent ftate of the Irifh commonalty, is intended to exafperate their feelings, or give a fhadow of countenance to their riotous and tumultuous meetings. There was a period when they had *lefs* reafon to be diffatisfied with their fituation than the prefent; and more has been effected towards meliorating their condition, during the laft ten years, than during preceding centuries. The almoft total repeal of the penal laws has completely reftored them to the rank and advantages of their fellow-fubjects. The corn bounties have brought to their doors a ready and profitable market for the produce of their farms; and the modification of the hearth tax has relieved numbers of the moft diftreffed from an affeffment, to them, grievous and heavy. If to thefe be added the improved and improving manners, and more enlarged ideas of their immediate fuperiors, and the milder treatment which muft neceffarily refult therefrom, the melioration in their circumftances, within fo fhort a fpace of time, will be found at once confiderable and progreffive. Then why, at fuch a period as the prefent, make public any remarks which *may* excite or counte-

nance

Another powerful engine which may be employed in the reformation of character, is Education;

tenance commotion and disturbance?—Because the evils we have noted, as before observed, though diminishing, still exist—their *complete* correction would prevent more efficaciously, perhaps, than any other circumstance, the returns of riot and disorder—and, to *expedite* such a reformation, it is surely necessary that the vices in question be made known, and generally understood. Besides, the *present* disturbances of the kingdom do not, to a certainty, arise from the oppression or other causes mentioned in the text, and which are in a state of progressive diminution; nor can they, it is presumed, be countenanced or increased by any remarks it contains. It is, indeed, to be feared, these commotions originate from other sources; from the machinations of the despicable few, who wish to overturn the happy constitution of these realms, and who push forward a wretched people, unconscious of the secret motives of such agitators, to the execution of the sword or of the halter. Fortunately, however, for our island, the arm of its government is sufficiently vigorous to quell such factious innovators; and, fortunately, the great majority of *Irishmen* are, indeed, *united* in steady opposition to their desperate councils. Nothing penned in the preceding pages can possibly countenance, if properly understood, the projects of such reformers; and if any of the positions laid down be erroneous, our errors are the mistakes of philanthropy, not the misstatements of sedition.

cation; of which an extenſive and applicable ſyſtem ſhould be introduced among our peaſantry; to whoſe other diſadvantages is added that of extreme ignorance, and no opportunity of information.

SECTION III.

On the beſt Means of providing Employment for the People of Ireland.

The moſt generally efficacious is the increaſe and diffuſion of capital—Reſpective value of Agriculture—Manufactures—Commerce.

HAVING briefly treated of the ſoil, ſituation, and productions of our iſland; and conſidered the general character of its inhabitants, and the moſt efficacious meaſures for correcting thoſe defects in it which may obſtruct their induſtry and employment; we are in this ſection to determine what are the beſt means of providing them with ſuch employment. We ſhall firſt premiſe ſome general conſiderations, and afterwards inveſtigate the ſubject under the ſubordinate heads of AGRICULTURE, MANUFACTURES, and COMMERCE.

It may be aſſumed as an axiom, that the induſtrious employment of any people muſt be proportioned, *cæteris paribus*, to the quantity of capital they poſſeſs. This will be ſo evident from conſidering that capital is the only fund for ſuch employment, from recurring to different pages of the firſt part of this Eſſay, and from conſulting the ſecond Book of Doctor Smith's profound Inquiry, that I ſhall not run the hazard of appearing tedious by adducing any additional arguments in its ſupport.

As capital, therefore, is the fund and ſource of employment, the moſt efficacious means of promoting this latter, eſpecially in any country where capital is deficient, muſt be thoſe which tend moſt to increaſe that capital. The general *diffuſion* of capital, likewiſe, among a people, appears a circumſtance eſſentially requiſite to the general promotion of employment. Where capital to a large amount is accumulated in the hands of a few, its beneficial influence in promoting employment cannot be near ſo extenſive, as where the ſame amount of capital is diffuſed among a greater number of proprietors.

It

It is the peculiar tendency of the mercantile ſyſtem to create ſuch an accumulation, to enrich a few at the expence of the majority, and frequently by the conflux of fleets, the ſumptuouſneſs of trading towns, and the ſplendour of the merchant, to give the appearance of general wealth and employment, while a conſiderable majority of the nation are, in a great degree, deſtitute of both. Such a partial accumulation of capital may be compared to a morbid congeſtion of blood in the human frame; its more general diffuſion, to the briſk and more equable circulation of health.

Ireland is a country in which capital is deficient, and in which the little capital ſhe is poſſeſſed of is partially and unequally diſtributed. The mercantile part of the community poſſeſs little, the agricultural ſcarcely any.

That branch of induſtry, therefore, which tends moſt forcibly at once to increaſe and equably diſtribute her general capital, is what ſhould be preferred and encouraged before any other. Such, preciſely, is *Agriculture*, which, independent

independent of its other numerous recommendations, already ſtated, is that from which the moſt ſpeedy, certain, and conſiderable increaſe of employment is to be expected. Her *Manufactures* are the next moſt important branch of induſtry. Her *Commerce*, though neceſſarily a valuable department, is that which ſhould laſt engage our concern. We ſhall inveſtigate the moſt adviſeable meaſures for increaſing the general employment of the people by theſe ſeveral meaſures, premiſing a few obſervations of Dr. Smith, on theſe ſubjects, which will give additional weight to the opinions we have advanced, and which are peculiarly applicable to the ſituation of our iſland.

" A particular country, in the ſame manner
" as a particular perſon, may frequently not
" have capital ſufficient, both to improve and
" cultivate all its lands, to manufacture and pre-
" pare their whole rude produce for immedi-
" ate uſe and conſumption, and to tranſport
" the ſurplus part either of the rude or manu-
" factured produce, to diſtant markets.

" When

" When the capital of any country is not " ſufficient for all theſe three purpoſes, in pro- " portion as a greater ſhare of it is employed " in agriculture, the greater will be the quan- " tity of productive labour which it puts in " motion within the country, as will likewiſe " be the value which its employment adds to " the annual produce of the land and labour " of the ſociety. After agriculture, the capital " employed in manufactures, puts into motion " the greateſt quantity of productive labour, " and adds the greateſt value to the annual " produce. That which is employed in the trade " of exportation has the leaſt effect of any of " the three.

" The country, indeed, which has not ca- " pital ſufficient for all theſe three purpoſes has " not arrived at that degree of opulence for " which it ſeems naturally deſtined. To at- " tempt, however, prematurely, and with an in- " ſufficient capital, to do all the three, is cer- " tainly not the ſhorteſt way for a ſociety, no " more than it would be for an individual, to " acquire a ſufficient one.—It is likely to in-

" creaſe

" creafe the faſteſt, when it is employed in the " way that affords the greateſt revenue to *all* " the inhabitants of the country, as they will " thus be enabled to make the greateſt fav- " ings. But the revenue of all the inhabitants " of a country is neceſſarily in proportion to " the value of the annual produce of their land " and labour. It has been the principal cauſe " of the rapid progreſs of our American colo- " nies towards wealth and greatneſs, that almoſt " their whole capitals have been hitherto em- " ployed in agriculture."

§ I. AGRICULTURE.

Proofs of its low ſtate in Ireland—from the appearance of the country—from inferiority of products—Cauſes of the inferiority of Iriſh agriculture—1. Want of capital—Proofs of this—Effects of the want of capital—2. High rent of lands—Calculation of the proportion paid by Engliſh and Iriſh tenants—3. Ruinous mode of ſetting lands in Ireland—4. Middle-men—Raiſe the rent of land—oppreſs the lower claſs, and are guilty of extortion and exaction—Do not improve the ſoil—Their exiſtence a proof of the backward ſtate of agriculture—5. Grazing—injurious to any country—Its ruinous effects in Ireland proved—From Mr. Young—From Dr. Campbell—Graziers monopolize land and raiſe the rent paid by the peaſantry—Low profits of grazing—Summary of the effects of grazing—Grazing not to be entirely deſerted—Vote of agiſtment—6. Tithe—7. Farming manufacturers—Injuries they occaſion—Modes of removing the impediments to agriculture, viz. 1. *Augmenting the capital of the immediate occupiers of the ſoil—*

2. *Altering*

2. *Altering the mode of ſetting lands—Advice to landlords on this ſubject—Practice has confirmed the juſtice of theſe concluſions*—3. *Securing an advantageous market to the farmer—Inland bounty—Bounty on the exportation of corn—Proofs of its good effects—Objections to bounties conſidered—Doctor Smith's chief objection—Anſwered—His objection, at any rate, inapplicable to Ireland*—4. *Abolition of tithe—Addreſs to the clergy on the ſubject—Generality of the clergy deſire the abolition—Objection to it anſwered—A better mode of raiſing the incomes of the clergy could be deviſed, and upon what principle*—5. *Grazing to be diminiſhed—Statutes to this purpoſe ineffectual—What is the effectual mode*—6. *Number of farming manufacturers, how to be diminiſhed—Agriculture to be directly encouraged, by the Dublin Society—Remarks on their premiums—County ſocieties recommended—Cultivation of barren lands to be encouraged.*

§ I. Agriculture.

IN investigating the moſt efficacious modes of advancing agriculture in Ireland, and conſequently the employment of her people, I ſhall conſider, firſt, the preſent agriculture of the kingdom, and the cauſes of its depreſſed and wretched ſtate; and, ſecondly, the beſt means of removing the defects and obſtructions to it which exiſt, and of promoting its general improvement.

The low and wretched ſtate of agriculture in Ireland requires little proof: even thoſe perfectly unacquainted with its practice, who have ſeen the rich and regularly cultivated fields of Flanders and England, muſt be convinced, from a glance, of its great inferiority. Mouldering fences, ſcanty crops, weeds univerſally prevalent, and a thouſand other ſimilar ſymptoms, evince it but too forcibly. Farmers by profeſſion, who have made more particular inquiries, give deciſive proofs that this inferiority is more than apparent.

rent. The annual products of a ſoil, fertile by nature, fall far ſhort of thoſe which the regular, opulent, and ſkilful huſbandman extracts from the earth in countries naturally more barren and unproductive. I ſhall content myſelf with one proof of this remark, from the Tour of the judicious Mr. Young. He draws the following averages of the products of England and Ireland:

England produces per Acre,

Wheat,	3 quarters	0 buſhels	0 pecks.
Oats,	4	6	0
Barley,	4	0	0

Ireland produces per Acre,

Wheat,	2 quarters	2 buſhels	3 pecks.
Oats,	3	4	3
Barley,	3	4	3

" The products, upon the whole, are *much* " inferior to thoſe of England, though not more " than I ſhould have expected, not from inferio- " rity of ſoil, but *extreme* inferiority of ma- " nagement."

" nagement." But even " They are not to be " considered as points whereon to found a full " comparison of the two countries; since a small " crop of wheat in England, gained after beans, " clover, &c. would be of much more import- " ance than a larger one in Ireland by fallow. " —Tillage in Ireland is very little understood. " In the greatest corn counties, such as Louth, " Kildare, Carlow, and Kilkenny, where are to " be seen many fine crops of wheat, all is un- " der the old system, exploded by good far- " mers in England, of sowing wheat upon a " fallow, and succeeding it with as many crops " of spring corn as the soil will bear."

The causes to which the inferiority of Irish agriculture is to be attributed are numerous. We shall investigate those in their operation most extensive, in their nature most injurious.

One of the most prevailing and powerful causes of the backward state of Irish agriculture is, the *want of capital* among the immediate cultivators of the soil. This want of capital is obviously evident from their wretched appearance,

pearance, and miserable modes of life. Behold the Irish husbandman sally forth to his work, barefoot and covered with rags: behold his ruinous hovel, built of mud, covered with weeds, and pervious to every shower that falls, and every pinching gale that blows. Behold him seated, after a hard day's labour, by a fire gleaned, perhaps, from the furze brake that overspreads his lands, involved in smoke, surrounded by a naked offspring, and sharing among them his dry and scanty meal. Look at his farm; a car thrown across a gap protects, in place of gates, the superior verdure of some reserved pasture; at which his lean horse, if such he possess, or starving cow, casts a hungry and desponding eye—his miserable crops are overrun with weeds; his temporary fences tumbling to decay; and every surrounding object, in short, affords convincing testimony of his extreme poverty. The want of capital among the Irish occupiers of land is equally evinced from considering the different motives to labour, by which they, and the more opulent farmers of other countries, are actuated. The Irish husbandman cultivates the earth merely to support existence.

As he expends no capital, he looks not to a return of profit. He expects no recompence for a life of labour, but the means of its prolongation. The English, or other opulent farmer, expects from his profession, not merely the recompence of his own labour, or the means of sustaining life, but the accumulation of profit proportionate to the amount of capital which he expends in its prosecution.

Agriculture, as well as every other branch of business, requires, to be carried to any degree of perfection, a fund or capital, which is at first expended in a variety of preliminary operations, without any immediate advantage, but which ultimately returns with accumulated profit. In England, no man thinks of taking a farm without a certain proportion of capital, and a stock of farming utensils. In Ireland, the wretched peasant will undertake the management of many acres without sixpence in his pocket, and no means of breaking and improving the stubborn glebe but the spade he carries on his shoulder. To remedy, as much as possible, these inconveniencies, he associates with others in a ſimilar ſituation. Thus endeavouring to ſupply the place of capital, and the various neceſſary apparatus of agriculture, by an union of the powers of that rude labour, which, if divided, muſt be ſtill more inadequate to the taſk it attempts to effect. Hence ariſes the deſtructive ſyſtem of taking large farms in partnerſhip; a practice in a great degree neceſſary, while the huſbandman is ſo abjectly poor and unprovided; but which always diſappears in proportion as he acquires capital, and conſequently the neceſſary mechanical implements of his profeſſion. At preſent, the poſſeſſion of the moſt neceſſary of all theſe implements, the plough, is, in ſeveral parts of the kingdom, by no means conſidered as eſſential to conſtitute a farmer: nay, even where a farm is taken by a number of wretched cottagers in partnerſhip, there frequently is not one in the whole colony. In general they ſcratch the ſurface of their corn lands with the ſpade, and where their fields are too extenſive for this management, perhaps there are half a dozen ploughs in a pariſh, the owners of which earn their livelihood by hiring them out by the day at a very high rate.

But how can any advances in the moſt important of all arts be expected from a people thus circumſtanced? As well may it be ſuppoſed that the ſavage, unacquainted with machinery and the mechanic powers, could ſucceſsfully imitate the moſt difficult exertions of the European, poſſeſſed of both.

Another cauſe which has frequently been mentioned, as deſtructive of the agriculture of Ireland, is the *high rent of land.* In conſidering this ſubject ſome difficulty occurs. Mr. Young, in his Tour, has given a calculation of the general rental of the kingdom from *hearſay*, which makes the acreable rent conſiderably below that of England. The average landlords rent of Ireland he makes, by this computation, 5s. 6d. Engliſh per Engliſh acre. The average landlords rent of England he calculated, in his different tours, to be 11s. 4d. per Engliſh acre. (See Appendix to his Tour.) The data on which this calculation of the Iriſh rental is founded, are, to any perſon acquainted with the average rental of different counties, evidently fallacious. I, for myſelf, am certain, that the average he gives of one

one county is below the truth. This, indeed, he acknowledges *may* be the cafe, and affigns reafons for fuppofing fo. As he traverfed, himfelf, the kingdom in different lines, and fets down in a table the rent, as well of the barren diftricts of Connaught, Kerry, and the Galtees, as of the fertile counties of Tipperary and Limerick; the minutes of his own journey form much more certain data for fuch a calculation. This calculation he has made, and the average rental *thus* obtained is 10s. 3d. per Englifh acre. Even this, however, is probably below the average rent paid by the immediate occupiers of the land, for the reafon he himfelf affigns. "The rents," fays he, "from which thefe particulars were "drawn, were not thofe paid by the *occupying* "tenant; but a general average of all tenures. "Whereas the object one would afcertain, is "the fum paid by the occupier, including, con-"fequently, not only the landlord's rent, but the "profit of the middle-man." But, farther, Mr. Young calculates as follows: "I have reafon to "believe that five pounds fterling per Englifh "acre, expended all over Ireland, which amount "to 88,341,136l. would not more than build,

"fence,

" fence, drain, plant, and improve that country, " to be upon a par in thofe refpects with England: and farther, that if thofe eighty-eight " millions were fo expended, it would take much " above twenty millions more, or above twenty " fhillings an acre, in the hands of the farmers, " in ftock of hufbandry, to put them on an " equal footing with thofe of her fifter kingdom. Nor is this calculation fo vague as " might at firft fight appear, fince the expences " of improvement and ftock are very eafily eftimated in both countries." If we wifh to know the real proportion of rent paid by the Englifh and Irifh farmer, this immenfe fum is to be taken into account. Let us calculate its annual intereft. The intereft of 6l. per acre at 6 per cent. per annum is above 7s. 2d. per acre. This, therefore, is to be added to the actual fum received by the landlord, if we wifh to afcertain the real proportion of rent paid by the Englifh and Irifh hufbandman. By this calculation the acreable rent of Ireland, if improved as England is, would be 10s. 3d. and 7s. 2d. or 17s. 5d. The acreable rent of England is 11s. 4d.

From

From the different mode of *setting lands* in England and Ireland, the proportionate rent must to a certainty be higher in the latter than in the former country. In England, when a lease is expired, the proportion of rent to be paid in future is amicably adjusted between landlord and tenant, according to a general principle almost universally adhered to, viz. that the landlord is to receive one-third of the whole annual produce as his rent. This, even, however, he seldom receives. I have seen a calculation, according to which the English farmer generally made four rents per annum, often five and six. From the prevalence of this mode of agreement between landlord and tenant, when a lease is expired, a third person scarcely ever interferes: the former occupier is supposed to have what is called a *tenant-right* to the premises. He is content to pay a reasonable advance for the improved state his farm may have arrived at; the landlord accepts the customary proportionate increase; and these customs, according to Smith, "so favour-"able to the yeomanry, have contributed more "to the present grandeur of England, than all "their

"their boaſted regulations of commerce taken
"together."

In Ireland, the mode of ſetting lands is perfectly oppoſite, and as deſtructive a ſyſtem of extortion as can be conceived. When a leaſe is expired, in place of ſuch an amicable adjuſtment, the lands are advertiſed to be let to the higheſt bidder, the propoſals of each are kept ſecret, and by this unfair ſpecies of auction, a promiſe of exorbitant rent is obtained, very frequently to the excluſion of the former occupier, who is conſidered as having no ſtronger claim to them than the moſt perfect ſtranger, unleſs he exceed him in the amount of the propoſed rent. This practice of *canting* lands, as it is termed, ſo univerſally prevalent, and ſo juſtly reprobated by every enlightened mind, proves ſeverely injurious to agriculture in two ways: by paying for his land an exorbitant and diſproportionate rent, the occupying farmer is kept in perpetual poverty, and prevented from acquiring that capital which would enable him to proſecute the cultivation of his farm more ſucceſsfully; and as the farmer is

certain

certain that any improvements made upon his land will but enhance their value upon the expiration of his leaſe, and from the competition of the cant neceſſarily and conſiderably raiſe his rent; if he inclines to continue an occupier, he neglects any except thoſe immediately neceſſary. Nay, he is tempted, as well from motives of preſent gain, as from the deſire of preventing others from outbidding him, to leave his farm in as ruinous a ſtate as poſſible. Hence ariſe thoſe clauſes in leaſes, ſo frequent in Ireland, preventing the occupier from turning up above a certain number of acres of ground during the laſt three years of his leaſe.

But theſe are not the only injuries occaſioned by the canting of lands; the evils are uſually repeated between the proprietor of the eſtate and the cultivator; and this leads to the conſideration of thoſe nuiſances *middle-men*, as they are termed. Theſe become the primary tenants to large diſtricts; and, dividing them into ſmaller, portion each out among the immediate occupiers and reſidents. Their only motive for taking theſe farms is the acquiſition of ſome annual pro-

fit.

fit. To obtain this, as they have probably become tenants at an exorbitant rent themſelves, they endeavour to gain ſuch profit by ſetting up the land among the wretched peaſantry to an auction ſimilar to that by which they themſelves obtained them. The farm is publiſhed, as it is called, at the chapel or market town. Private propoſals are to be made, and no preference to be expected, except by the higheſt bidder. Attached, from various motives, to the place of his reſidence, and having little proſpect of bettering himſelf elſewhere, as every acre of land in his vicinity is probably in the hands of ſimilar jobbers, the former proprietor is tempted to offer an extravagant rent, from the dread of being ouſted from his little dwelling, by ſome more bold ſpeculator. To this inconvenience, however, notwithſtanding his advanced offers, he is frequently obliged to ſubmit. A higher bidder is often at hand, who ſupplants the former wretched tenant, and either drags out a miſerable exiſtence under a diſproportionate burden, or failing in the endeavours to diſcharge his promiſes, drives off his ſtarving cattle, in the night, to ſome diſtant and

mountainous

mountainous diſtrict, and is no more heard of by his diſappointed landlord.

But middle-men are injurious to the agricultural intereſts of Ireland in more ways than we have juſt mentioned. They are the claſs from whom the poor principally experience that oppreſſion, to which we have aſſerted they are ſtill ſubject. A middle-man, poſſeſſed of large farms, and reſident among his tenantry, can, and too frequently does, act the deſpot over them without the ſemblance of reſiſtance. Many of them have no leaſes but at will, but even thoſe who have obtained a tenure of twenty-one or thirty-one years, are ſtill liable to be turned out at the whim of the landlord; for although he may not be ſo daring as to attempt illegally to diſpoſſeſs them, yet by driving their cattle when the rent falls due, and harraſſing them in a variety of ways, he will compel them either to unlimited ſubmiſſion, or a voluntary ſurrender of their premiſes. By theſe means, and by the ſcandalous connivance of magiſtrates and juries, where a *gentleman* is in queſtion, the middle-man poſſeſſes an uncontrouled dominion over his vaſſals; and

thoſe

thoſe who know human nature will be but too ſenſible how liable ſuch a poſſeſſion is to abuſe.

Beſide the exorbitant rent which he engages to pay, the wretched tenant, in conſequence of this power, is liable to further exactions from the reſident middle-man. Is his maſter's turf to be cut and drawn home, the gratuitous ſervice of himſelf and horſe is expected. Are the gentleman's crops to be ſaved, although his own are rotting, and the ſcanty wages of labour, from a preſs of buſineſs, are ſomewhat raiſed in the neighbourhood, his attendance at the cuſtomary rate is expected, and expectation is enough. Does his lady want the luxury of eggs for breakfaſt—— but it would be diſguſting to deſcend to a detail of pitiful exactions, the very recital of which ſhould raiſe the bluſhes of every petty lordling conſcious of their perpetration.

An improvement in the agriculture of the kingdom might be hoped for from middle-men reſident in the country, and, in their own defence, neceſſitated to practiſe ſome degree of huſbandry. Vain are ſuch expectations. A general

improvement

improvement in agriculture will never be effected by gentlemen-farmers. Their hufbandry differs little from that of the cottagers who furround them; their profits, in place of being fo ufefully employed, are expended in idle diffipation and extravagance. The yell of a pack of ftarving beagles is more pleafing to their ears than the fong of the ploughman. The fight of their fellow fportfmen, drenched to infenfibility in whifkey, more pleafing to their eyes, than luxuriant crops, and well cultivated fields. They are the clafs among whom what remains of the ferocious fpirit of drinking, which formerly difgraced the kingdom, is ftill to be found; they are thofe from whom principally emanate all the bad confequences we have already afcribed to oppreffion, diffipation, extravagance, and pernicious example.

As the exiftence of an intermediate tenant between the poffeffor and immediate occupier of the foil, is a circumftance which, in the various ways we have mentioned, obftructs and depreffes the agriculture of Ireland; fo it affords an additional proof, befide thofe already given, of the low ſtate of that important branch of employ-ment. Middle-men are only known in the un-improved parts of every empire. In the central and well cultivated ſhires of England they do not exiſt; in the diſtant and poorer diſtricts there are ſome traces of them. In Scotland they are common; in Ireland they are wearing out in the more rich and beſt cultivated counties; in thoſe of a contrary deſcription they are almoſt univer-ſal. In France the ſame obſervations are appli-cable. In ſhort, their number and frequency are in every country in an inverſe ratio to its wealth and improvement.

Another diviſion of the landholders of Ireland, who contribute conſiderably to the depreſſion of agriculture, are the *graziers*. With reſpect to diſ-ſipation, extravagance, and oppreſſion, this claſs are pretty much on the ſame footing with the middle-men we have juſt noticed. The branch of buſineſs they purſue is pregnant with addi-tional obſtacles to the cultivation and improve-ment of this or any other country where they are numerous. It would be as tedious as unne-ceſſary to enter into a particular detail of the va-

rious

rious modes by which the general practice of grazing muſt injure any country in which it predominates. The univerſal coincidence of political writers in their ſentiments, as to its injurious tendency, precludes the neceſſity of any ſuch minute diſcuſſion. That its prevalence in Ireland has not been more propitious than elſewhere is generally allowed, and might be eaſily demonſtrated, even from the very appearance of thoſe counties in which it moſt prevails. The agriculture and general face of the country is ſufficiently poor, even in thoſe diſtricts of Ireland where tillage is moſt attended to and beſt underſtood; but its miſery takes a ſtill deeper hue in thoſe counties naturally more fertile, where their fields are devoted to paſturage. For this, out of many others, take the teſtimony of two modern travellers. Mr. Young, ſpeaking of the rich grazing lands of the county of Limerick, ſays,

" In no part of Ireland have I ſeen more care-
" leſs management, than in theſe rich lands, the
" face of the country is that of deſolation; the
" grounds are overrun with thiſtles, ragwort,
" &c. to exceſs; the fences are mounds of earth
" full

" full of gaps; there is no wood, and the general countenance is ſuch, that you muſt examine into the ſoil before you will believe that a country which has ſo beggarly an appearance can be ſo rich and fertile."

The other authority I ſhall quote is that of Doctor Campbell. On approaching Munſter, the grounds "aſſumed," ſays he, "a very different appearance from what I had before obſerved. The inauſpicious effects of paſturage became, however, viſible before I left Leinſter. For ten or twelve miles on this ſide of Kilkenny the ſoil was far from rich; it was rather, indeed, poor; yet it was pretty well cultivated: the fields were encloſed with hedges and ditches, and the country embelliſhed with houſes and plantations. But as the ground improves, on approaching the borders of Munſter, agriculture ceaſes, and not a houſe or a hedge or a ditch is to be ſeen; the country is abdicated by the human ſpecies, and peopled with ſheep."

Graziers,

Graziers, by taking and monopolizing large tracts of land, and covering them with ſheep and bullocks, not only conſiderably diminiſh the population they would naturally have arrived at, but render the ſituation of the few wretched peaſantry who do remain attached to the ſoil, infinitely more miſerable than that of thoſe who inhabit leſs fertile diſtricts. It is an obſervation which muſt ſtrike every traveller through Munſter, where grazing chiefly prevails, that the greater the fertility of the ſoil, the more wretched are the peaſantry who occupy it. The cottager who ſtruggles againſt nature on the barren mountain's ſide, is more comfortably circumſtanced, than he whoſe poſſeſſions lie in diſtricts exuberantly rich by nature. This is chiefly occaſioned by the exorbitant rents the latter are obliged to pay in conſequence of the extenſive monopolies of graziers. Where the land is naturally ſo fertile as to yield ſpontaneouſly a profuſion of rich herbage, ſufficient to fatten the largeſt cattle, without the ſmalleſt exertion of agricultural labour, the rich and indolent grazier, ſatisfied if he can obtain a light profit upon each acre, with little trouble and attention, bids a high rent for,

 and

and obtains very extenſive tracts; and either excludes entirely the labouring peaſant, or re-lets to him a few acres at a further profit rent. But in thoſe diſtricts where nature is leſs propitious, and where the exertions of *ſome* labour and induſtry are abſolutely requiſite to extract *any* profit from the ſoil, the peaſant, freed from ſuch powerful competitors, obtains his land at ſomewhat a cheaper rate, and is enabled, of conſequence, to effect greater improvements, and to live more comfortably, than the inhabitants of the moſt fertile diſtricts, on whom the bounty of nature operates as a curſe, not a bleſſing.

Graziers are almoſt the only occupiers of the ſoil in Ireland who poſſeſs any conſiderable capital. It requires a very large ſum to ſtock an extenſive fattening farm. The profits, however, ariſing from grazing, are beneath all due proportion inconſiderable. Mr. Young calculates, that the ſum neceſſary to ſtock a bullock farm is ſix pounds an acre, and that the annual profit, after all deductions, is but eight ſhillings and ſeven-pence, which is very little more than the legal intereſt of the money at ſix per cent. without

out taking into account the rifk of lofs of cattle, bad markets, &c. Although we are not to credit this calculation, it could be proved to a demonftration, that a profit infinitely fuperior to that really gained might be procured by properly employing the fame capital in agriculture. Why then does not felf-intereft lead the grazier into its practice? He is prevented by ignorance and indolence. The improved modes of agriculture he is unacquainted with; and were he bleffed with the information, the comparative flothful eafe he at prefent enjoys would not eafily be forfaken for a more lucrative branch of bufinefs, which demanded greater exertion and attention.

Many, therefore, and powerful are the impediments to employment which grazing occafions. It diminifhes population; it promotes indolence. The extenfive capital it requires, which in any other occupation would give work to thoufands, fupports but a few wretched and flothful herdfmen. As the profits of grazing are fmall, it diminifhes the annual augmentation of national capital, which otherwife would be accumulated.

As it checks and impedes the progreſs of agriculture, it depreſſes that branch of buſineſs from which we have ſhewn the moſt extenſive, ſecure, and beneficial ſource of employment is to be expected.

Let it not be imagined that we would recommend a total deſertion of grazing. Many large tracts in this iſland, as we have already hinted, are calculated for nothing elſe. Beſides, the general purſuit of agriculture does not, by any means, include the total neglect of fattening. On the contrary, it is evident that, in all extenſive countries, and eſpecially in Ireland, whoſe climate is ſo favourable to paſturage, the univerſal and ſpirited practice of agriculture will, by the general introduction of artificial roots and graſſes, at preſent almoſt unknown, increaſe the number of cattle fattened, and lower the price of butchers meat; while, at the ſame time, its fields will become populous, and the employment of their inhabitants beneficial and extenſive.

The preſent ſyſtem of grazing in Ireland, though ſo pernicious, is not a little encouraged by grazing lands being generally exempted from tithe. This is in confequence of a vote paffed by the Houfe of Commons in the year 1735, called the *Vote of Agiftment* ; by which it was refolved, " That the demand of tithe agiftment " for cattle was grievous and burdenfome,—that " all legal ways and means ought to be made " ufe of to oppofe all attempts for carrying de- " mands for fuch tithe into execution, &c." An exemption of this nature operates as a bounty on pafturage, and a tax on agriculture; and it is manifeftly unjuft that the latter fhould bear the entire burden of fupporting the clergy, and the former not contribute a farthing. This leads us to the confideration of another obftacle to the agriculture of Ireland.

Tithe. Much of what might be advanced on this head has been anticipated in the former part of this Effay. It has been there fhewn, that any tax of this nature muft confiderably impede the advancement of agriculture in any country, and under any circumftances. But fuch a tax muft be peculiarly deftructive in its operation when agriculture is in a ftate of infancy, and where

where thofe who practife it labour under many other additional oppreffions and inconveniencies. This is peculiarly the cafe in Ireland, where this branch of induftry fhould receive every encouragement, and be relieved as much as poffible from every burden. Many facts have been lately advanced in our Senate, and many publications iffued from our prefs, refpecting the peculiar feverity with which tithe has been exacted in different parts of this kingdom. From the political fituation of the Irifh peafant he muft be more expofed to exaction, than the more rich and independent farmers of other countries *; but

* It is difficult to form a calculation of the comparative amount of tithe in Ireland and England. There are fome data for it in the average rates of Englifh and Irifh tithes given by Mr. Young; the amounts per acre for corn are very fimilar, and therefore Mr. Young fays they "afford no proof that tithes in Ireland are "unreafonably rated." He feems to forget the table of produce he before gave (fee page 247). If the produce is much lefs in Ireland, and that produce much lefs advantageoufly obtained, a fimilar acreable rate is certainly a heavier burden in Ireland than England, more efpecially when we take into account the difference of quality and the different money price of that produce in the twc

but I ſhall not enter into an invidious recapitulation of the aſſertions which have been advanced, in which much truth and much miſrepreſentation have, as is uſual upon ſuch occaſions, been induſtriouſly combined. I reſt the queſtion entirely upon *general* principles; and content myſelf with recapitulating, that tithe in kind, however collected, muſt in every ſituation repreſs and obſtruct agriculture; and that it muſt be peculiarly ruinous where that occupation is ſtruggling againſt poverty, oppreſſion, and ignorance. Such is its ſituation in Ireland; and if the ſkilful, opulent, and independent Engliſh farmer finds the

tax

two countries. Let us take the article wheat as an inſtance. If a quarter of Engliſh wheat ſells for 30s. in England, a quarter of Iriſh will not be worth 26s. in Ireland. But let us ſuppoſe this the proportion:

An Engliſh acre yields 3 quarters at 30s.	£.	4	10	0
An Iriſh, ſay - - 2¼ at 26s.		2	18	6

The average wheat tithe of England is 4s. 11d. per acre, that of Ireland 4s. 2½d. See Young, page 55.— The Iriſh peaſant, therefore, out of 2l. 18s. 6d. pays 4s. 2½d. tithe; the Engliſh, out of 4l. 10s. 0d. but 4s. 11d. The average tithe of hay, according to Young, is in England 1s. 10d. in Ireland 2s. 0d.

tax peculiarly inconvenient, oppreſſive, and burdenſome, with how much greater ſeverity muſt it gall the poor and ignorant and oppreſſed peaſant of our iſland?

In the manufacturing parts of Ireland, and particularly in Ulſter, the progreſs of agriculture is conſiderably injured by every manufacturer being poſſeſſed of ſmall portions of land, and acting both as a farmer and artizan. The diviſion of labour, and confining the exertions of workmen to one particular branch of buſineſs, as it affords a proof of the conſiderable progreſs of any ſociety in opulence and civilization, ſo it increaſes the ſkill and dexterity of the workman in whatever ſpecies of labour he is ſolely employed; and tends to augment his capital more rapidly than can be effected by a varied and deſultory attention to a diverſity of occupations. A contrary plan diminiſhes both the productive powers and profits of the artiſt. "The advan-"tage," ſays Smith, "which is gained by ſav-"ing the time commonly loſt in paſſing from "one ſort of work to another, is much greater "than we ſhould at firſt view be apt to imagine.

"It

" It is impoſſible to paſs very quickly from one " kind of work to another, that is carried on " in a different place, and with quite different " tools. A country weaver, who cultivates a " ſmall farm muſt loſe a good deal of time in " paſſing from his loom to the field, and from " the field to his loom. A man commonly ſaun- " ters a little in turning his hand from one ſort " of employment to another; and this renders " him almoſt always ſlothful and lazy, and in- " capable of any vigorous application even on " the moſt preſſing occaſions."

The evil conſequences of a combination of occupations are unfortunately felt in their utmoſt extent in the North of Ireland. The agriculture of the country has been particularly and deeply injured by its prevalence. Of this ſtronger proofs cannot be given than thoſe contained in the obſervations of Mr. Young. " View the " North of Ireland; you there behold a whole " province peopled by weavers: it is they who " cultivate, or rather beggar the ſoil, as well " as work the looms. Agriculture is there in " ruins; it is cut up by the roots; extirpated,

" annihilated.

" annihilated. The whole region is the diſgrace " of the kingdom. All the crops you ſee are con- " temptible, are nothing but filth and weeds: " no other part of Ireland can exhibit the ſoil in " ſuch a ſtate of poverty and deſolation. But " the cauſe of all thoſe evils, which are abſolute " exceptions to every thing elſe on the face of " the globe, is eaſily found. A moſt proſperous " manufacture, ſo contrived as to be the de- " ſtruction of agriculture, is certainly a ſpectacle " for which we muſt go to Ireland. It is owing " to the fabric ſpreading over all the country, " inſtead of being confined to towns;—there, " literally ſpeaking, is not a farmer in a hun- " dred miles of the linen country of Ireland. " The lands are infinitely ſubdivided; no weaver " thinks of ſupporting himſelf by his loom; he " has always a piece of potatoes, a piece of oats, " a patch of flax, and graſs or weeds for a cow; " thus his time is divided between his farm and " his loom.——Where agriculture is in ſuch " a ſtate of ruin, land cannot attain its true va- " lue; and, in fact, the linen counties, propor- " tioned to their ſoil, are lower let than any " others in Ireland.—If I had an eſtate in the " South of Ireland I would as ſoon introduce

" peſtilence

" peſtilence and famine upon it as the linen " manufacture, carried on as it is at preſent in " the North of that kingdom †."

Having

† In ſome converſation had with Doctor Burrowes, reſpecting the injuries which *farming manufacturers* occaſion to agriculture, he expreſſed very ſtrong doubts whether the deſcription given by Mr. Young, and which we have juſt quoted, was not highly exaggerated. It is but juſt to inform the reader, that the opinions advanced on this point reſt on the authority of Mr. Young *alone*; and that in general our remarks on the Northern parts of this kingdom are derived almoſt entirely from the information of others. Thoſe on the Southern are more the reſult of perſonal obſervation. The only ground on which the exiſtence of farming manufacturers appears defenſible was at the ſame time ſtated by Dr. B. viz. the ſuperior degree of health which ſuch workmen muſt enjoy, compared with thoſe accuſtomed to conſtant confinement; and he mentioned that he had himſelf lately obſerved the moſt ſtriking contraſt between the ſqualid, pale, and ſickly artizans of Mancheſter, and other parts of England, and the robuſt weavers of Ulſter. Whether the injuries aſcribed by Smith, Young, and others, to this combination of profeſſions, are counterbalanced by the ſuperior health reſulting therefrom, muſt be left at preſent to the reader's determination, who will alſo be, from this note, better enabled than before to appreciate the value due to different remarks on the Northern parts of Ireland, which the text contains.

Having pointed out the moſt conſiderable impediments to the progreſs of Iriſh agriculture, we are next to inveſtigate the moſt efficacious modes to be purſued for its advancement and improvement. The moſt prominent object, in ſuch inveſtigation, muſt be the removal of thoſe obſtructions which we have detailed; in what manner this object can be beſt attained, is, therefore, firſt to be examined.

The radical and moſt efficacious obſtruction to the improvement of agriculture in Ireland is the prevailing and conſiderable deficiency of capital among the immediate occupiers of the ſoil. This deficiency will be found, on examination, either immediately or remotely the conſequence of the different partial impediments we have above enumerated. The introduction and general diffuſion of a greater degree of wealth among the occupying peaſantry muſt form the baſis of any ſolid improvement in their modes of cultivating the earth.

The firſt and moſt efficacious ſtep which could be taken towards bettering the ſituation of the

farmer

farmer, in this reſpect, would be a general alteration in the mode of ſetting him his land. The average rental of Ireland we have ſhewn, conſidering the relative improvement of the two countries, to be conſiderably higher to the tenant than in England. We have alſo proved that this ariſes from the pernicious mode in which lands are let; and it is evident a very conſiderable portion of the rent thus exacted from the poor goes into the pocket of the middle-man, and is productive of no advantage to the owner of the eſtate. The proprietors of land, therefore, ſhould ſolemnly and univerſally determine never to ſet to any perſon but an occupying tenant; they ſhould for ever aboliſh the ruinous cuſtom of canting lands; they ſhould allow the tenant a reaſonable profit, and be content with a reaſonable rent; and ſhould never loſe ſight of the noble idea of tenant-right, which in England has been ſo religiouſly attended to, and is ſo immenſely beneficial. I am well aware how difficult it is to eradicate national habits, eſpecially in an inſtance of this nature, where the revenue of the individual might, from ſuch an alteration, be ſuppoſed liable to conſiderable diminution.

minution. But I am equally well convinced, that the more intimately the ſubject is inveſtigated, the more evident will it appear, that the conſideration of private intereſt, as well as of public advantage, ſhould equally lead the perſons concerned to adopt the plan of conduct we have recommended; and that thereby their incomes would be ultimately and ſecurely increaſed. What is the advantage to the landlord, of allowing a certain portion of his rent to be abſorbed by the rapacious middle-man? The only feaſible argument which can be offered in defence of the practice, is, that his rent is better ſecured by ſuch intervention. But even this ſuppoſition is abſurd. If arrears be due, to what mode of enforcing payment had the landlord beſt reſort? to the perſon of the *gentleman*, who, perhaps, will anſwer any importunate demands by a challenge or defiance, or to the ſtock of the occupying peaſant? Surely to the latter; and to that, in ſuch caſes, does he always ultimately recur. But although the proprietor of land ſhould determine to let to none but the occupying tenant, little advantage will accrue to the farmer, if he ſets it by auction to the higheſt bidder, without

any

any attention to the old resident, or without allowing him a reasonable interest in the tenement. An allowance of this nature, may, to the short-sighted, appear too great an exertion of self-denial, too considerable a sacrifice of property, to be made from patriotic motives with any degree of prudence. But those who form such conclusions do not look far enough; they calculate from the amount of rent, which, by the present mode of setting lands, is extorted from a starving and miserable people, without taking into consideration the increase which might be obtained from them, without either injury or injustice, by persisting in a contrary plan. Allow your tenant a reasonable profit; enable him to accumulate some capital; he will then pursue agriculture on an extensive and advantageous scale; he will necessarily employ it in the occupation to which he has been bred; and consequently improve the land, from which, by your novel but prudent encouragement, he has extracted the means of its improvement. Give him but a comparatively short lease; at its expiration demand a moderate rise of rent; it will be cheerfully granted. Let the increase be equitably propor-

tioned

tioned to the improvement of the farm; but let not ſuch improvement be rendered an engine of extortion, or the means of expelling from your poſſeſſions the man who has ſo much contributed to increaſe their value. By perſevering in ſuch a plan of conduct, your eſtates will in a few years aſſume a different appearance from that of their preſent ſtate of deſolation; their improvement, and the rent they afford, will equally and conſiderably increaſe; and you will, at the ſame time, feel the inexpreſſible felicity of beholding an opulent, thriving and comfortably ſituated tenantry of your own rearing, and reap the ſolid advantage of increaſing, without oppreſſion or extortion, the amount of your annual income. The landlord who allows his occupying tenantry an intereſt of the nature we ſpeak of may be conſidered as laying out yearly a ſum equal to the difference between a moderate and a rack rent, which ultimately returns to himſelf with compound and accumulated profit, and which has, in the mean time, enriched the perſon entruſted with its management.

The rent of land has, it is true, confiderably increafed in Ireland, notwithftanding its wretched management, and the ruinous plan purfued in fetting it. But this rife has been the confequence of the increafed price of its products, not of the improvement of the foil. Had a contrary fyftem been adopted, the augmentation would at this day be much more confiderable; it would have increafed both by the rife of prices and by improved cultivation.

Thefe conclufions are not the refult of mere abftract and theoretic fpeculation. The experiment has been tried; it has fucceeded. In England, from the high ftate of its cultivation, refulting from the liberal mode of fettlement purfued between the proprietor and occupier of the foil, rent, though lower to the tenant, is higher to the landlord than in Ireland; and, what is of equal confequence, it is fecurely and punctually paid. A few partial and ifolated inftances of the fame nature have occurred in Ireland; and, wherever fairly tried, have been fuccefsful. Were they univerfal, their beneficial confequences to both parties would be ftill more confiderable.

Mr. Young records a happy inſtance of this nature in the conduct of Sir William Oſborne; and a ſimilar plan has been purſued by the amiable Sir George Saville. It is related by Dr. Campbell, in his 32d Letter.

From the cuſtom which prevailed formerly all over Ireland, of ſetting leaſes of large tracts for ever, or for a long period of years, to middlemen, they have, from the increaſe of prices, obtained ſo conſiderable a profit in the ſoil, that they may be conſidered, with reſpect to inferior tenantry, in the ſame light as the original proprietors of the eſtate. Its improvement would be the immediate intereſt of ſuch tenants, though of no advantage whatever to thoſe from whom they derive their leaſes; and, in letting to the occupying tenantry, they ſhould purſue preciſely the ſame line of conduct which we have recommended to landlords of another deſcription.

Next to the equitable and mutually advantageous mode of agreement between landlord and tenant, which we have juſt recommended, the moſt effectual mode of increaſing the capital, and improving

improving the hufbandry of the latter, is fecuring a fteady and profitable market for his productions. One very efficacious expedient for this purpofe is the erection of flour mills in convenient parts of the country. Many of thefe, upon an extenfive fcale, have been built within a few years, and their number is daily increafing.

Whatever may be the defects and difadvantages of the *inland bounty* on flour carried to Dublin (fee Young's Tour), it certainly has been fo far beneficial as to have occafioned the erection of a number of mills which would otherwife have never been attempted, and of thereby fecuring, and bringing to the farmer's door, a ready market for the chief of his productions. Mr. Young afferts, that this inland bounty has proved very prejudicial to Ireland; that it has diminifhed its pafturage exports, and introduced and extended a wretched and execrable tillage. However deficient and unfkilful the agriculture introduced may be, its very introduction muft be confidered as a beneficial circumftance; as the capital of the farmer increafes it will improve, and is improving. With refpect to the

 benefit

benefit or injury derived to the kingdom at large by the inland bounty, the balance ſtruck by Mr. Young between agricultural and paſturage exports and imports affords no ſolid ground for any opinion. The nature of the occupation encouraged by this bounty, and the circumſtances of thoſe with whom it ultimately reſts, the farmers, he leaves entirely out of the queſtion. As to the promotion of employment, the advantage of having agriculture in any way encouraged in preference to paſturage, admits of no doubt. Twenty acres under tillage will afford greater occupation than twenty times twenty grazed by ſheep and bullocks.

But the moſt effectual of all expedients which have yet been deviſed for ſecuring a ſteady and beneficial market to the farmer, is the *bounty on the exportation of corn.* Bounties have been known in Ireland ſince the reign of Queen Anne, but they were either inadequate, ill contrived, or counteracted. The Iriſh bounty act deviſed by Mr. Foſter, and ultimately ſettled in the year 1784, ſeems happily calculated to ſecure a ſettled demand for the ſeveral ſpecies of corn, to encou-

rage

rage their growth, and to prevent at all times their high price or ſcarcity. The beneficial influence of corn bounties has been particularly experienced in Ireland. Not many years ſince ſhe depended for a ſufficient quantity of grain on importation, and was ſupplied principally by England and America. Its exportation was either ineffectually encouraged, prohibited, or permitted only in a deſultory manner by ſtarts and intervals. The conſequence was, as in every other ſimilar inſtance, that the farmer, not being certain of a ſteady and advantageous market, neglected raiſing a ſufficient ſupply of ſo neceſſary an article, and the country, notwithſtanding a conſiderable import, very frequently experienced conſiderable want. The bounty has at once produced a certain market for the farmer, increaſed the average price of ſome of his products, and ſecured an abundant ſupply of corn for home conſumption. This muſt be evident to the moſt ſuperficial inquirer.

Before the year 1780, though ſome bounties were granted by 29 Geo. II. and other acts, they were ill deviſed and ineffectual; and we conſtantly ſtartly imported large quantities. In that year the firſt efficient bounty act took place, and the ſtate of the corn trade for five years ending Lady-day 1785 was as follows:

	£.	s.	d.
Value of corn, ground and un-ground, exported from Lady-day 1780 to Lady day 1785	705822	11	2¾
Value of corn, ground and un-ground, imported during the ſame period - - -	624940	12	7
Balance in favour of export -	80881	18	7¾

In the year 1785, the improved bounty act, paſſed the preceding year, began to operate. The account of five years from Lady-day 1785 to Lady-day 1790 is as follows:

	£.	s.	d.
Value of corn, ground and unground, exported during theſe five years - -	2204162	18	11¼
Value of the ſame articles imported during the ſame period - - -	37225	7	3
Balance in favour of export -	2166937	11	8¼

So

So confiderable an increafe in production and demand, occafioned both by the bounty on inland carriage to Dublin and on export from every port, muft have augmented the profits and general capital of the farmer. Its beneficial operation has, to be fure, been confiderably counteracted by the ruinous mode of fetting lands, and the other exactions we have mentioned, which are in general too ftudioufly made to keep pace with any fuch augmentation. Still, however, they have in fome degree produced the effect. The agricultural tenantry have in feveral counties increafed in number and in wealth; fome little improvement in their modes of tillage is obfervable; and the fyftem which has produced even the fymptoms of fuch an alteration of circumftances fhould be ftudioufly adhered to.

The utility of bounties has, I know, been arraigned by many, and efpecially by fo refpectable an authority as Doctor Smith. I mean not to queftion any obfervations of his on other bounties; but as his authority muft neceffarily carry great weight, and as I confider the continuation of corn bounties as one of the great means of encouraging agriculture, at leaft in Ireland,

Ireland, and confequently of effectually promoting the employment of the people, a fummary of his objections to them, as far as refpects the ftate of this country, and an examination of their validity, cannot be deemed irrelevant to the queftion before us.

It is not my intention to enter into a minute inveftigation of this fubject. Many of Doctor Smith's arguments have been anfwered in a fatisfactory, and others in a confufed manner, by Mr. Anderfon, in his Obfervations on National Induftry. P. S. to Letter XIII. to which, and Doctor Smith's work, Book IV. Chap. V. I refer the reader for a more particular examination of the queftion. With refpect to Ireland, it cannot for a moment be doubted, that the bounty on exporting corn has confiderably increafed its production, that it has introduced a more regular fupply than was before known, and that it has turned a greater number of hands to Agriculture than were before employed in it. The moft fuperficial retrofpect to the ftate of the kingdom for fome years back muft afford irrefragable proof of the truth of thefe affertions. In thefe refpects

its

its beneficial influence has, from experience, been found confiderable and extenfive.

The moft weighty and ingenious objection of Doctor Smith to corn bounties we fhall give an abridgement of in his own words. " That " in the actual ftate of tillage, the bounty on " exportation neceffarily tends to raife the mo- " ney price of corn in the home market, will " not be difputed by any reafonable perfon— " the corn bounty, therefore, as well as every " other bounty on exportation, impofes two " different taxes upon the people, firft, the tax " which they are obliged to contribute in or- " der to pay the bounty; and, fecondly, the tax " which arifes from the advanced price of the " commodity in the home market; and as the " whole body of the people are purchafers of " corn, this fecond tax is by much the heavieft " of the two.—So very heavy a tax upon the " firft neceffary of life muft either reduce the " fubfiftence of the labouring poor, or occafion " fome augmentation in their pecuniary wages, " proportionable to that in the pecuniary price " of their fubfiftence. So far as it operates in " the

" the one way, it muſt reduce the ability of the " labouring poor to educate and bring up chil- " dren, and muſt ſo far tend to reſtrain the po- " pulation of the country. So far as it operates " in the other, it muſt reduce the ability of the " employers of the poor to employ ſo great a " number as they otherwiſe might do, and muſt " ſo far tend to reſtrain the induſtry of the coun- " try. The enhancement of the money price of " corn, however, it has been thought, by ren- " dering that commodity more profitable to the " farmer, muſt neceſſarily encourage its produc- " tion. I anſwer, that this might be the caſe if " the effect of the bounty was to raiſe the *real* " price of corn, or to enable the farmer with an " equal quantity of it to maintain a greater num- " ber of labourers in the ſame manner, whe- " ther liberal, moderate, or ſcanty, that other " labourers are commonly maintained in the " neighbourhood; but neither the bounty, nor " any other human inſtitution, can have any " ſuch effect.—The money price of corn regu- " gulates that of all other home-made commo- " dities; it regulates the money price of labour " —the money price of all the parts of the rude " produce of land—and, conſequently, that of

" the

" the materials of almoſt all manufactures. " Though, in conſequence of the bounty, there- " fore, the farmer ſhould be enabled to ſell his " corn for four ſhillings the buſhel, inſtead of " three and ſixpence, and to pay his landlord " a money rent proportional to this riſe in " the money price of his produce; yet, if in " conſequence of this riſe in the money price of " his corn, four ſhillings will purchaſe no more " home-made goods of any other kind than " three and ſixpence would have done before, " neither the circumſtances of the farmer, nor " thoſe of the landlord, will be much mended " by the change."

In conſidering the validity of this objection, two circumſtances are to be principally conſidered; firſt, Does the bounty on the exportation of corn enhance its price in the home market? and, ſecondly, Does ſuch enhancement produce all the evil conſequences attributed to it?—The natural tendency of any bounty on exportation is confeſſedly to raiſe the home price of the article exported. It is not eaſy to imagine how the bounty on corn would, in this reſpect, operate differently

differently from that on any other article, except by giving riſe to a greater production. Certain, however, it is, that ſince the inſtitution of bounties the average price of corn has fallen in England. This Doctor Smith ſuppoſes has happened *in ſpite* of the bounty; but his reaſoning on this head is far from ſatisfactory. In Ireland, the ſame event has in ſome meaſure taken place. The price of wheat laſt year, notwithſtanding the very conſiderable export, was much more moderate than for many preceding ſeaſons. The operation of the Iriſh bounty on oats has been different; it has nearly doubled its price in a few years; and, for reaſons to be hereafter ſtated, I conſider ſuch riſe as a favourable circumſtance. But even allowing the exportation bounty increaſes ſomewhat the average price of all kinds of corn, any inconvenience reſulting from ſuch riſe is more than compenſated by its producing a regular and ſteady ſupply of the home market, and preventing the oppoſite evils of profuſe abundance or alarming ſcarcity. Doctor Smith ſuppoſes that bounties do not produce even this effect, but, on the contrary, that by forcing an exportation they prevent the ſuperabundance of

one

one ſeaſon from relieving the ſcarcity of another. His objections on this ground, however, have been very fully anſwered by Mr. Anderſon. Bounties, ſo far from occaſioning, have proved the moſt effectual means of preventing ſcarcity. A retroſpect to the hiſtory of ſcarce years, and embargoes, will prove this very fully ; and Mr. Anderſon very well illuſtrates their mode of operation in this way, as follows :

" Let us ſuppoſe that the greateſt variation in " the total amount of the crop between a year " of the greateſt plenty and one of the greateſt " ſcarcity, amounts to *one-fourth* of the whole " crop. Let us again ſuppoſe that the ordinary " and conſtant export did, in years of medium " plenty, amount to *one-eighth* of the whole pro- " duce, the farmer would in this caſe be in the " conſtant practice of rearing *one-eighth* more " grain than ſupplied the inhabitants in ordinary " years ; ſo that when the crop, through the " unfavourableneſs of the ſeaſons, fell ſhort of " its ordinary quantity *one-eighth* part, there " would ſtill be enough in the country to ſup- " ply the internal demand, as *the eighth* part of

" it

" it that was destined for exportation would " exactly supply the deficiency. No importation " would, therefore, be needed in this case. But " if, instead of *one-eighth* or one-sixteenth, the " usual quantity exported should have amount- " ed to *one-fourth* of the whole crop in ordinary " years, it would follow, that in the greatest " scarcity that could ever happen from bad sea- " sons, there would still remain *one-eighth* for " exportation, after the deficiency occasioned " by the bad crop was fully supplied.—So far, " therefore, is the exportation occasioned by the " bounty from hindering the plenty of one year " from relieving the scarcity of another, as Dr. " Smith supposes, that it is, perhaps, the only " method which can be devised for effecting that " purpose with any degree of laudable œcono- " my.—As to the supposition, that farmers would " ever be induced to rear more grain than was " necessary for supplying the demand in years of " tolerable plenty, and that they would make a " common practice of retaining the surplus quan- " tity in their possession till a year of scarcity " should come, I frankly own that the idea of " it appears to me extravagantly absurd."—

But

But even ſuppoſing, with Doctor Smith, that bounties do in general conſiderably raiſe the money price of corn, and of conſequence the wages of labour and price of all manufactured produce; his reaſonings, though deſerving conſiderable attention in other countries, are not by any means applicable to the preſent ſtate of Ireland. The fundamental poſition on which all his concluſions are founded, is, that corn, being the principal univerſal article of ſubſiſtence, is that whoſe price muſt regulate that of every other article of production or manufacture. Mr. Anderſon aſſigns many reaſons for ſuppoſing this is by no means univerſally the caſe; it certainly is not in Ireland. By far the moſt material article of ſubſiſtence among the great maſs of the community here, eſpecially among the agricultural peaſantry, is the potatoe. Corn they conſume little of, and, among us, it, therefore, cannot be that regulating article which Doctor Smith ſuppoſes it in every inſtance. It is here to be conſidered in the ſame light as rape, or any other article for export, produced by the farmer. Nay, further, the ſteady and advanced price, and the conſequent increaſed cultivation and export of corn, occaſioned by bounties,

ties, instead of enhancing the value of the prevailing articles of subsistence, potatoes, renders them both more plentiful and cheaper than they were before the bounty took place, or than they would be in case it were abolished. For potatoes are very generally the meliorating crop first employed in breaking up the soil and preparing it for the production of every species of corn. The export bounty, therefore, as being, at least with respect to Ireland, free from the inconveniencies which have been attributed to it, as tending to increase the profits, and consequently augment the capital of the farmer, as encouraging the cultivation of the earth, and as diminishing the pernicious prevalence of pasturage, we hesitate not to pronounce one of the most effectual expedients which can be devised for removing many impediments to, and extending the prosecution of agriculture, and consequently of efficaciously and beneficially promoting the general employment of the people.

Next to the bounty on the exportation of corn, which has been tried with so much increasing success, perhaps there is no measure which

which would more effectually promote the agriculture of Ireland than an alteration in the mode of paying the ſalaries of the clergy.

I ſhall not offer any additional arguments in ſupport of thoſe already advanced, to prove that tithe is a tax pernicious, impolitic, and oppreſſive. Its injuries are too glaring, and have been too uniformly felt and acknowledged to require more minute proof, or to demand a more particular anſwer to each flimſy argument advanced in its favour; and I cannot bring myſelf to think, that it is not in the power of human ingenuity to deviſe a leſs exceptionable mode of raiſing a fund neceſſary for the maintenance of the miniſters of religion. I am aware that any alteration in the mode of levying the eccleſiaſtical eſtabliſhment has, by many of the clergy, been deemed dangerous; and that any propoſal to that effect may be ſuppoſed to proceed from an enemy to their order. But if the matter be properly conſidered, it will appear very evident, that the clergy ſhould be more anxious than any other deſcription of people to promote an alteration ſo anxiouſly deſired. I accuſe them not of exaction; I charge them not as an enemy; I speak to them as a friend; and I think there are considerations which press with peculiar force upon the ministers of the gospel, and should render them especially desirous for the abolition of this tax. What can be in itself more improper, what more distressing to a feeling and a religious man, than to be forced to receive his subsistence, in a great measure, from a class of people whose industry is their only support, and to many of whom, in this country, he renders not any benefit to entitle him to a participation in the hard-earned fruits of their labour and fatigue? What more disagreeable than to receive this subsistence by scanty and remote payments, to obtain even which he is frequently obliged to have recourse to means which nothing but necessity could excuse to his own heart, and which involve him in feuds and contentions with those whose amity and good-will he ought and must be desirous to cultivate? I speak not of the alternative of a tithe-farmer—to adopt the practice would in general but increase the difficulties of the parishioner, and, consequently, I should hope, the uneasiness of the pastor; and where a clergyman does not set his tithes thus, is it fit, I will

ask,

aſk, that he ſhould devote ſo large a portion of his time, as the viewing and ſetting of his pariſh will neceſſarily require, to ſuch employments? Can ſuch occupations be pleaſing to a gentleman, to a man of liberal education, and refined taſte? Is it fit that, by a ſeeming mercenary attention to ſums, which, though trivial in themſelves, are neceſſary to his ſupport, he ſhould be obliged to run the riſk of being accounted unfeeling and avaricious, by thoſe whoſe good opinion he ſhould be ſtudious to merit and obtain? May not the habit of attending to petty bargains, and counteracting the artifices and ſleights employed by the farmer, to leſſen a tax he thinks it a hardſhip to pay at all; may not the vexations which muſt occur in the courſe of ſuch tranſactions, and the quarrels and litigations which enſue, narrow the ſoul, and weaken or exclude the affections, that dignify human nature, and ſhould glow with uncommon fervour in the breaſt of the Chriſtian divine?

Theſe, and other conſiderations we have advanced, have at length opened the eyes of many of the clergy themſelves, as to their real in-

 tereſts,

terefts, and induced them to wifh for fome alteration in the mode of collecting their ftipends. I never fpoke on the fubject to any liberal-minded and well-informed individual of the profeffion who was not a ftrenuous advocate for a radical alteration of the fyftem. The public and fevere reprobation of tithes, contained in the moral philofophy of the venerable Archdeacon Paley, are a proof of the fentiments of the moft enlightened of the clergy refpecting this inftitution, and fhould carry confiderable weight with thofe ftill defirous of adhering to fo ruinous an inftitution.

It has been afferted, that the abolition of tithe would be productive of no effential fervice to the occupying tenantry of this kingdom, as their landlords would raife their rents in proportion to the amount of fuch exemption. That rents would be raifed is to be expected; that they would not be raifed to the full amount of the value of tithes at prefent levied, I am certain. A tenant would never agree *a priori* to pay in a round fum an addition to rent equal to what is extracted from him for different articles of his produce, from a defire

defire of avoiding the difagreeable interference of others in the collection and management of his crops, and from a variety of other motives. But even allowing rents were raifed to the full amount of rent and tithe, as at prefent collected, ftill the alteration would be attended with material advantages. The tax would then be ftable and certain, and no longer variable, and proportioned to the labour and fkill, the improvement and induftry of the farmer; evils the moft pernicious of any attendant on this eminently deftructive fyftem.

It has been prefumptuoufly afferted, that no alteration in the mode of collecting their revenue could be devifed, which would not be attended with material difadvantage to the clergy, and particularly that in no other way could their falaries be always augmented, in fair proportion to the rifing wealth and improvement of the country. I fhall not here enter into the refpective merits of the many plans for fuch alteration which have, within a few years, been offered to the public. I am confident it would be eafy to devife a mode free from the very many in-

conveniencies

conveniencies of the present, and even more beneficial to the clergy themselves.

In the dominions of the king of Prussia, and in Bohemia, Sardinia, and the Milanese, a land tax is assessed according to an actual valuation of the ground, which varies its amount according to the rise and fall of the value of land, by the latter undergoing a valuation at particular periods. It appears extremely possible to devise, on similar principles, a mode of collecting a church revenue, equivalent to that at present produced by tithe, free from its inconveniencies, and so calculated as to increase with the rising prosperity of the country. It is not the object of the present Essay to enter into a particular discussion of this subject, else we think it might be shewn, that such a plan could be carried into execution with greater facility, and less expence, than might at first view be imagined, and that it would be attended with considerable advantages to all parties concerned. Oppressive as the tax, in its present form, confessedly is, were the whole of its amount calculated, and levied upon all lands without distinction, whether pastured or tilled, according to their value, which might be determined by parish juries, the acreable assessment of the whole kingdom would be very light, and even if paid by the landlords, would be ultimately of considerable advantage to them. " The tithe," says Smith, " where " there is no modus, and where it is levied " in kind, diminishes more what would other- " wise be the rent of the landlord, than a land " tax which really amounted to five shillings " in the pound." By a system of this nature, the destructive impediments to agriculture resulting from tithe would be removed; the iniquitous inequality occasioned by the vote of agistment corrected; and the maintenance of the ministry of the gospel no longer prove the source of oppression to the people, of poverty to the nation, and of feuds, contention, and litigation between those who should be united in the bonds of amity, harmony and peace.

Grazing we have shewn to be a very destructive impediment to the progress of agriculture, and there is none which more effectually obstructs the employment of a people. The diminution

nution of its prevalence, therefore, becomes an important object. To attempt effecting this by prohibitory ſtatutes would be an arbitrary, unjuſt, and ineffectual meaſure. Of this we have an inſtance in the hiſtory of Engliſh grazing. In the reign of Henry VII. paſturage was ſo generally prevalent, and the evils ariſing from it ſo evident, that he enacted a ſtatute againſt it. Yet the miſchiefs continued to increaſe ſo conſiderably, that Henry VIII. to check its progreſs, carried the penal clauſes former ſtatutes contained into execution. The decay of tillage, and increaſe of paſturage, however, became ſo univerſal, and the evils felt by the people from the latter ſo grievous, that they abſolutely roſe in rebellion in the reign of Edward VI. deſtroying the property and puniſhing the perſons of the obnoxious. A commiſſion was appointed to inquire into the cauſe of theſe riots; and their report was, that they were occaſioned by converting arable into paſturage grounds; ſo that where twenty or two hundred people formerly lived, nothing was then to be ſeen but ſheep and bullocks. Further ſteps were taken to prohibit theſe practices, and ſomething more was attempted ed in the reign of Elizabeth, but little or nothing accompliſhed.

The moſt effectual and unobjectionable mode, perhaps, to check and diſcourage grazing, is to promote and encourage agriculture. When it is evident that the profits of the latter are much ſuperior to thoſe which can be acquired by the former, it will attract the ſtock and attention of the grazier, in ſpite of habitual predilection and long confirmed indolence. The export bounty, therefore, by ſecuring and increaſing the profits of tillage, ſeems happily calculated to diminiſh grazing, and it has in fact already produced that effect;—many tracts of ground, not long ſince deſtined for fattening, have been lately turned up, and the practice is daily ſpreading. Still it is extraordinary that few poſſeſſed of capital are ſeen to employ it in the proſecution of improved, ſcientific, and extenſive agriculture. Although tillage has increaſed, eſpecially in Munſter, conſiderably, it is ſtill carried on, as uſual, in the old deſtructive mode, and by perſons poſſeſſed of neither capital or ſkill. This appears in a great degree the conſequence of of ignorance as to the improved practice of agriculture, and of the profits which result from it. If we can pay any attention to agricultural calculators, and even if we make large deductions from the profits which they state to arise from particular branches of skilful tillage, it should attract more capital than it yet has done in our island. But even the present alteration from pasturage to tillage must be considered as extremely beneficial. The capital of the farming part of the nation is daily increasing; their skill will increase with it, and ultimately arrive at some degree of perfection; and, at any rate, the employment of the people has been, even already, promoted by the change.

Another circumstance, which would tend considerably to diminish pasturage, would be the equable assessment of the church revenue on all lands in proportion to their value. The present mode of collecting it, and the exemption of pasturage grounds from any share of the load, operates as a tax on tillage and bounty on grazing. The mode of collection we have hinted at would completely annihilate this inequality; and, as grazing grounds are in general the richeſt and moſt valuable in the kingdom, they would very juſtly bear a conſiderable ſhare of that burden which at preſent oppreſſes agriculture alone.

We have mentioned another impediment to the extenſion and improvement of tillage, which exiſts principally in Ulſter, and which ſhould be ſeriouſly attended to, viz. the multitude of farming weavers, or weaving farmers, which overſpread the country. A more effectual mode cannot, perhaps, be deviſed than that recommended by Mr. Young, who was ſo ſenſible of the injuries they occaſion to agriculture. "The "landlords of the country might, with no great "difficulty, effect the change: let them ſteadily "refuſe to let an acre of land to any man that "has a loom. The buſineſs would and ought "to be gradual; but farms ſhould be thrown "by degrees into the hands of real farmers, and "the weavers driven into towns, where a cab"bage-garden ſhould be the utmoſt ſpace of "their land. All encouragement, all attention, "all bounty, all premium, all reward, ſhould "go

" go to thoſe alone who lived by and attended
" to their looms, not in a ſeparated cabin, but
" in a ſtreet;——and if, contrary to common
" ſenſe, a paltry board is permitted to exiſt,
" by way of promoting a fabric of two mil-
" lions a year, let them have this object, and
" this only, for their buſineſs. Let them deviſe
" the means of inducing landlords to drive their
" weavers into towns, and they will in a few
" years do more good to their country than all
" their inſpectors, itinerant men, and ſpinning-
" wheels, will do in a century *."

Such are the principal obſtructions which impede the agriculture of Ireland, and ſuch appear the moſt efficacious meaſures which can be adopted for their correction or removal, and the conſequent promotion of the employment of the people. So great is the native and intrinſic vigour of the occupation, that it would require little other aid than freeing it from the difficulties with which it has been encumbered. Still, however, it may be promoted, not only by the removal

* See Note, page 251.

removal of theſe obſtructions and impediments, but by direct encouragement. Let us examine what meaſures of this nature had beſt be purſued.

In the conſideration of this ſubject, the Dublin Society naturally take the lead. Backward as the agriculture of Ireland is, this juſtly celebrated body have not a little contributed to advance it, even to its preſent ſtate. Their premiums have introduced many beneficial modes of huſbandry, which, though not generally followed, are increaſing, and will gradually become prevalent without the extraordinary aid of bounty. From their long attention, they may naturally be ſuppoſed better acquainted with the beſt modes of promoting the intereſts of the kingdom at large than any individual; yet a few general obſervations on the line of conduct they had beſt purſue may not be deemed impertinent. The Society, as their charter expreſſes, were inſtituted for the purpoſe of promoting agriculture. To this important object their attention ſhould ever be principally directed. It cannot, however, eſcape obſervation, that they ſome years back did

did deviate more and more from the original defign, paying particular attention to and making many ftrong attempts at forcing different manufactures. Little, however, has in this way been effected; and it will tend more to the advantage of the kingdom if the original intention of the inftitution be principally kept in view, and the greateft proportion of their funds employed in the encouragement of agriculture.

Many of the premiums propofed and paid by the Society are very judicioufly devifed; yet one idea they have adopted fhould be more generally attended to and practifed than yet appears to be the cafe. I mean diftributing many fmall premiums among the poor, inftead of a few confiderable ones among the gentlemen farmers. Any general or confiderable advances in agriculture are never to be expected, except from a numerous, fubftantial, fkilful, and independent yeomanry. Thofe can only be raifed from the prefent poor, oppreffed, and ignorant, though improving peafantry of our ifland. To them, therefore, fhould all encouragement be principally and fkilfully directed. A number of fmall premiums, properly and conſtantly diſtributed among them, would increaſe both their capital and ſkill, and excite them to improvements at preſent utterly neglected. A few premiums to a large amount, given to a few gentlemen, for conſiderable exertions, which require a large capital, no doubt, cut a ſtriking figure when related, and have their uſe, nor ſhould they entirely be deſerted; but ſuch exertions are very frequently the effect of the whim and caprice of the moment, or the deſire of diſtinction; they are uſually deſultory, and lead to no very general, ſtable, or ſyſtematic improvement in our agriculture. A perſeverance in a contrary plan, though leſs brilliant in appearance, will ultimately be much more beneficial, and lead to more generally diffuſed, and more ſolid advantages.

Not only the diviſion, but the nature of the premiums propoſed, would ſeem to require ſome alteration. The implements and materials of improvement ſhould be given as rewards. Ploughs and harrows, and horſe hoes, and hoe-ploughs, and a variety of other machines, might be diſtributed, and their employment encouraged. Premiums

miums are ſometimes offered for the culture of different articles, the very ſeed of which the poor Iriſh peaſant is not able to purchaſe. An inſtance occurs in clover; a premium per acre has been held out for its cultivation, to be paid the ſubſequent year; but how can the poor farmer pay five or fifteen pounds in the ſpring ſeaſon for clover ſeed, and remain out of it for twelve months, even though certain of obtaining the premium? If you wiſh to be uſeful, give the ſeed to any who apply for it, on proof of their intention to claim the premium, and purſue the mode of cultivation recommended; let a bounty be ſuperadded, to the moſt ſucceſsful, and let a warehouſe, for theſe and ſimilar purpoſes be opened in each county. Innumerable inſtances of this nature might be pointed out; but they muſt inevitably ſtrike the good ſenſe of the Society, if they only adhere to the principle of improving the occupying peaſantry, and of adapting their premiums to the ſkill, ſituation, and circumſtances of thoſe whom it ſhould be their principal object to aſſiſt and enlighten.

County ſocieties, for the improvement and encouragement of agriculture, might be eaſily inſtituted, with conſiderable benefit. The men of landed property would ultimately find it conſiderably to their advantage to promote ſuch inſtitutions, and to diſtribute annually, from a ſmall fund, which might eaſily be collected, ſuch premiums as they ſhould deem moſt calculated for improving and aſſiſting their tenantry. Scotland affords, in ſome degree, an example of this nature; premiums to the moſt ſkilful ploughmen are adjudged and diſtributed annually in ſeveral parts of that kingdom. The plan might eaſily be improved upon, and the trifling ſubſcriptions neceſſary to carry it into execution would ſurely be more advantageouſly and rationally laid out than in plates to racers or contributions to hunting clubs.

Another meaſure for promoting the agriculture of the kingdom would be the encouraging the cultivation of barren lands. Such ſhould at leaſt be tithe free for a certain number of years: and it is ſurpriſing the clergy ſhould oppoſe an exemption which muſt ultimately prove advantageous to themſelves †. Parliament ſhould alſo attend to this ſubject; ſome of the conſiderable ſums expended on bounties to manufactures, or ſtill more intereſted private jobs, would be much more advantageouſly directed in this channel.

† Barren lands are, by an act paſſed this ſeſſion, made tithe free for ſeven years after their firſt cultivation.

§ II. Manufactures.

Reference to principles established in Part I.—Linen manufacture—Defects in the mode of conducting it—Pecuniary assistance afforded to it disproportionate and unnecessary—Absurdity of endeavouring to extend it all over the kingdom—Causes of our deficiency in other manufactures—Want of capital—Commercial restraints under which we laboured for many years—Historical sketch of these restraints—On the woollen manufacture—Injustice of them—Examination of the compact—Similar restraints imposed on other manufactures—Injuries they occasioned to our manufactures—Other bad effects resulting from them—Their removal—Expectations formed upon this event—Why were not manufactures immediately established and improved—Consideration of the applicability of the usual expedients for improving manufactures—1. Free exportation—2. Bounties; Objections to them—3. Prohibiting the importation of manufactures—Impolicy of this measure—Advantages of the home manufacturer—These advantages

vantages sufficiently great—Another objection to protecting duties—No exception against the general impolicy of such measures exists in Ireland—They should, therefore, be rejected—4. Prohibiting the exportation of materials—Wool—No alteration in the regulations as to its export necessary—5. Prohibiting the exportation of materials in any stage of manufacture short of the last—Yarn—Impolicy of restraining its export—Importance of the manufacture of linen yarn—Importance of the manufacture of woollen yarn—Reduction of interest—Advice to manufacturers—Present state of Irish manufactures—Woollen manufacture—Cotton manufacture—Glass manufacture—Paper manufacture—Silk manufacture—Conclusion.

§ II. MANUFACTURES.

NEXT to agriculture, manufactures are the moſt important object of attention in any country, and the moſt fertile ſource of employment. It would be needleſs to enter into any calculation of the numbers which, in thoſe countries where manufactures flouriſh, are variouſly occupied in them. The multitudes to which they afford employment, and their very great importance to any ſtate, are too evident, and too univerſally admitted, to require either proof or illuſtration. We are here principally to conſider the moſt adviſeable modes of increaſing and extending the manufactures of Ireland, and, conſequently, of providing employment for her people.

It is unneceſſary here to recapitulate the modes recommended by the agricultural ſyſtem of political œconomy, for introducing and extending manufactures in any country, which have gained ſo great a degree of approbation from the deepeſt political

political writers. An abridgement of them will be found in the first part of this Essay, and a more minute account in the works to which we have there referred. But although the means which this system recommends should always be held in view, and pursued as far as prudence will admit, they cannot be implicitly followed in the present state of European nations, involved, as they are, in a labyrinth of monopolies, bounties and prohibitions. Keeping a steady eye upon them, however, and at the same time considering those more usually adopted, and the relative situation of Ireland, as to external connection, we shall investigate the best means of introducing new, and extending her old manufactures.

The linen manufacture of Ireland is the foremost object of the present article, and is, indeed, almost the only branch of which she has been for many years possessed. It has received the particular attention and assistance of Parliament, through the medium of the board of trustees, who first met in the year 1711, and whose exertions in its favour have been unremitting ever

since.

ſince. The manufacture has flouriſhed, and is flouriſhing to ſuch a degree, that any obſervations reſpecting the beſt modes of further encouragement may be deemed ſuperfluous. The proofs are already in the hands of the public. The exportation has progreſſively and conſiderably increaſed, and the proportionate importation of the primum, and its ſeed, have diminiſhed. The tables which afford the moſt concluſive proof of theſe aſſertions may be eaſily obtained, and need not here be recapitulated.

Notwithſtanding, however, the flouriſhing ſtate of the manufacture, the mode of conducting and extending it does not appear altogether free from faults. The very deſtructive practice of allowing the weavers to ſpread over the country, and to attend to two occupations at a time, has been already noticed; and the impediments it occaſions to agriculture pointed out. For the reaſons there aſſigned, the manufacture itſelf muſt be injured by it; and would, conſequently, be ſerved, as well as the agricultural, and general intereſts of the country, by drawing them into towns, and confining their exertions to one particular

ticular branch of bufinefs. The means of doing fo have been already ftated.

It cannot efcape obfervation, that the linen manufacture has been fupported and extended at a very confiderable expence to the nation. The duties appropriated to this purpofe, and the bounties paid by Parliament, have amounted to between thirty and forty thoufand pounds per annum. Although fuch extraordinary encouragement may be requifite to an infant and ftruggling manufacture, it can fcarcely at prefent be neceffary to one fo long and fo firmly eftablifhed as that of linen in Ireland. All great manufactures, as thofe of wool and hardware in England, and of filk in France, require and enjoy no fuch extraordinary aid. Demand is all that is neceffary to render them flourifhing; that demand Ireland is eminently in poffeffion of, and I am fatisfied that, if the immenfe fums we have mentioned were at prefent withdrawn, and directed in more neceffary channels, the manufacture would flourifh, and prove as beneficial as ever to the nation.

Another

Another erroneous idea respecting the linen manufacture is, that of the necessity and utility of forcing its extension all over the kingdom. This is absurd. It is well observed by the author of 'The Commercial Restraints of Ireland 'considered,' "That no populous and commer- "cial country can subsist on *one* manufacture. "If the world ever produced such an instance," says he, "I have not been able to find it." The endeavours of the board to extend this manufacture to the southern provinces have been ineffectual. The want of capital, and other circumstances, have rendered of no effect all the temptation of bounties and premiums. Capital, however, is increasing. Let those possessed of it employ it in the manufactures they find most likely to prove advantageous. Let Parliament, if they please, encourage their infant exertions; but let them not persist in the pernicious plan of endeavouring to turn every manufacturing hand in the kingdom to the linen loom.

If we except that of linen, Ireland possesses, as yet, no manufacture of any very considerable extent or importance. One principal cause of

this

this deficiency has been the prevailing want of capital; many sources of which we have already traced, and whose deleterious consequences in other instances we have before had occasion to lament. This want of capital is one of the most powerful obstacles to the establishment or improvement of manufactures they can possibly encounter. The Scotch, though possessed of very good wool, and enjoying all the advantages of English manufacturers, cannot work it up for want of capital (See Smith and Anderson). The want of capital has ever been felt in this kingdom. Inconsiderable as were the little foreign trade and manufactures carried on in 1672, nearly half the stock which supported them belonged, according to Sir William Petty, to foreigners. At another period, Lord Strafford says, the whole trade of the kingdom was carried on by Dutch capitals; and, at present, a considerable portion of the capital which supports business is English. To divert a greater proportion of the general wealth of the country, amassed in the hands of individuals, and employed by them, either in loans, the funds, or totally unemployed, towards manufactures and trade, the Parliament of Ireland

land have, by a ſtatute, permitted any perſon to inveſt a certain portion of his property in company with others in any branch of buſineſs, without ſubjecting the remaining part to the claims of any creditors of the partnerſhip, or to the operation of the bankrupt laws; with the proviſo, that the ſum ſo appropriated to buſineſs be publicly regiſtered. This exemption has, no doubt, prompted many to employ ſome portion of their capital in manufactures and trade, which would not otherwiſe be ſo directed; but ſtill it cannot, in any very conſiderable degree, diminiſh the general national deficiency of capital.

The augmentation of this capital, as well as the eſtabliſhment or advancement of any other manufacture, ſave that of linen only, was effectually prevented for a ſeries of years, by the reſtraints, equally unjuſt and impolitic, under which our iſland laboured till within a very ſhort period. A *brief* ſketch of the origin and operation of theſe reſtraints cannot be deemed foreign to the ſubject before us; this we ſhall firſt delineate. We ſhall afterwards inquire, why the relaxation of them has not as yet given riſe to any very important

portant or extenſive fabric: we ſhall next inveſtigate the beſt modes to be purſued for extending and improving the manufactures of the kingdom; and conclude with an examination of their preſent ſtate.

The blind and ſelfiſh ſpirit of commercial jealouſy, which frequently outwits itſelf, and ultimately injures thoſe intereſts it is deſirous of ſolely aggrandizing, has been the parent of thoſe reſtrictions on the induſtry of Ireland, whoſe baneful influence was ſo long felt, and which, after their extinction, is even ſtill protracted. However Ireland might have been injured in other reſpects, the promotion of her manufactures appears to have been as much an object with the Engliſh government, as that of their own, from the period of firſt enacting any ſtatutes reſpecting them, to the year 1663. The ſtatute-book is replete with inſtances of this nature. Whenever any meaſures are enacted for extending the manufactures of England, Ireland is generally included; and whenever the importation of foreign manufactures is prohibited, there is always an exception in favour of thoſe of Ireland.

land. In the year 1663 the firſt diſtinctions commenced, by the prohibition contained in an Engliſh act, 15 Cha. II. chap. 7. againſt the exportation of a variety of articles from Ireland to the Plantations; but the year 1669 may be dated as the commencement of thoſe reſtraints which, during the ſubſequent century, depreſſed or annihilated the manufactures of this country.

The woollen manufacture had been, for many years before this period, eſtabliſhed in Ireland; it had been encouraged by a variety of Engliſh acts; and although, as might naturally be expected from the poor and diſturbed ſtate of the country, the advances in it were, comparatively ſpeaking, trivial; ſtill an exportation to ſome amount had been made, and was daily increaſing. A reſolution was entered into by the Iriſh Houſe of Commons in the year 1695, "to ap-"point a ſelect committee to prepare heads of a "bill for the better making and regulating the "woollen manufacture of the kingdom." This, and the gradually riſing ſtate of the manufacture, alarmed the jealouſy of our commercial neighbours; and on the 10th of June 1698, an ad-

dreſs

drefs was prefented by the Houfe of Lords in England to the King, containing a requeft, that his "Majefty would be pleafed, in the moft "public and effectual way that might be, to de-"clare to all his fubjects in Ireland, that the "growth and increafe of the woollen manufac-"ture there had long, and would ever be looked "upon with great jealoufy by his fubjects of "England, and if not timely remedied might "occafion very ftrict laws, totally to prohibit "and fupprefs the fame." His Majefty's anfwer was, that he would take care to do what their Lordfhips defired. An addrefs, in ftrong terms, was prefented by the Commons, on the 30th of the fame month; and part of his Majefty's anfwer thereto was, "I fhall do all that in me lies "to difcourage the woollen manufacture in Ire-"land." The intentions of the Englifh admi-niftration were communicated to the governing powers of Ireland; their influence, as it muft be confeffed has fince been too frequently the cafe, was fuccefsfully exerted to prevail on Parliament to adopt meafures the moft deftructive to the interefts of their conftituents; an act was introduced and paffed, laying an additional duty

of

of four ſhillings for every twenty ſhillings value of broad cloth exported from Ireland, and two ſhillings for every twenty ſhillings value of new drapery, except frizes. This, however, did not ſatisfy the Engliſh, and accordingly a law was paſſed in England, prohibiting, from the 29th of June 1699, the exportation from Ireland of all goods made of or mixed with wool, except to England and Wales, where duties had been before laid on importation equal to prohibition. By this act, and one or two that followed, a total end was put to the woollen trade of Ireland. Though in its infancy, it was at that period the principal manufacture of the kingdom—it did even then afford employment to many—it would, in its progreſs, have afforded it to ſtill greater numbers; and, as the nation was in itſelf poſſeſſed of the neceſſary primum, it was that in which the greateſt advances and improvement were naturally to be expected. The plea, advanced at the time, in extenuation of reſtrictions ſo evidently unjuſt and injurious, was, that the linen manufacture was to be encouraged in and monopolized by Ireland; while the woollen manufacture was, by theſe and other regulations, to be confined to England. I ſhall not enter

enter into an examination of the evident injuſtice of depriving a nation of a manufacture for which they were naturally calculated, and in which they were making advances; and forcing them to adopt another, of which they poſſeſſed not the primum, and with which they were comparatively unacquainted. Nor ſhall I enter into a minute examination of the degree of faith with which Great Britain adhered to the terms of this compact *, as it has been improperly termed. All theſe circumſtances have been very well illuſtrated, in that excellent pamphlet, "The Commercial Reſtraints of Ireland conſidered," to which we muſt refer thoſe deſirous of more particular information on this head.

With

* The compact has certainly been violated by Great Britain in many particulars. She has prohibited the importation of chequed, ſtriped, printed, painted, ſtained or dyed linens of the manufacture of Ireland. She has encouraged, by ſeveral meaſures, the linen manufacture in Scotland, and to that degree that 17074777 yards were ſtamped for ſale there in 1783. She has laid a duty on ſail-cloth imported from Ireland into England, and ſhe has granted bounties on the exportation of Britiſh chequed and ſtriped linens, while the terms of the *compact* diſadvantageous to Ireland were rigidly adhered to.

With refpect to other manufactures, the fame fyftem of depreffing all of Irifh growth, by preventing exportation, was gradually effected. The Englifh poffeffions in America and the Weft Indies were among the beft and moft natural marts to which we could refort for the difpofal of any articles of this nature. But thefe, by feveral ftatutes, were fhut againft us, while our own markets were laid open to an inundation of Englifh manufactured produce. Other markets, either by particular acts * or lefs direct expedients, we were prohibited from reforting to; and, by thefe devices, domeftic confumption was the only fource of encouragement left to our artifts in every branch of manufacture but one.

A more effectual expedient (if we except only direct prohibition) could not, perhaps, be devifed for depreffing or annihilating the manufactures of a country. Although the home market

* The Irifh having made fome progrefs in the glafs manufacture before the 19th Geo. II. were, by an act paffed that year, prevented from exporting to any country, or fo much as lading a carriage with it with intent to export.

ket be, in many inſtances, the moſt advantageous and important to manufactures, it is not in all; and freedom of exportation ſeems indiſpenſably requiſite to the advancement of any to a ſtate of perfection. Whether this be owing to that emulation which competition in foreign markets gives birth to, to the increaſed demand which exportation naturally occaſions, or to theſe combined with a variety of other cauſes, it is not very material to determine. Experience has ſufficiently proved the juſtice of the concluſion, whatever may be the ſources to which we may trace the effect.

Baneful, indeed, were the conſequences of theſe unjuſtifiable reſtrictions. The impediments under which agriculture laboured, and which we have already ſtated, prevented any accumulation of riches by that occupation. The reſtraints at preſent under review, effectually deprived the people of the means of any ſimilar acquiſitions by manufactures. The two great ſources of national wealth being thus completely obſtructed, any accumulation of national capital was completely prevented. This deficiency neceſſarily

ceſſarily deprived them of the means of making any advances in either branch of buſineſs, of relieving the general poverty under which the kingdom ſtruggled, or of affording employment to the lower and labouring claſs of the community.

The patience of an oppreſſed and declining people being at length exhauſted, the nation was rouſed, at a favourable opportunity, to a reſiſtance to that oppreſſion under which, for a century, they had with unexampled patience acquieſced. The Parliament of Ireland, which met the 12th October 1779, in an addreſs to his Majeſty, ſtated, that a free trade alone could ſave the nation from impending ruin. The Houſe of Lords concurred in ſimilar expreſſions, and their ſentiments were, at leaſt on this occaſion, thoſe of the people at large. It is unneceſſary to enumerate the different circumſtances which at this period concurred to give efficacy to the repreſentations of Parliament; ſuffice it to ſay, that the Engliſh miniſter deemed it eligible to comply with the demands of the nation, and that bills were, in December 1779, brought into the

English Parliament and passed, by which the laws which prohibited the exportation of any woollen manufactures from Ireland to any part of Europe, and those which prohibited the exportation of glass from Ireland, were repealed; and the Irish were at the same time permitted to export and import commodities to and from all parts of America and the British colonies in the West India Islands and Africa, subject to such regulations as should be *adopted* by her own Parliament. The attainment of these advantages extended the views of the people, and led to the acquisition of others even more important. They considered that as long as England retained the power of making laws to bind this country, the relaxation she had concurred in was a boon revocable at pleasure, and that, as at a former, so at some future period, commercial jealousies might prompt her to retract what she considered, not as a right, but an indulgence. These and other motives more strictly *constitutional* gave rise to the subsequent exertions and demands of the Irish people, which were at length satisfied by the settlement of 1782, when the sole right of Ireland to regulate her commerce,

merce, and bind herſelf in all caſes, was fully recognized.

Thus, after the lapſe of ſo many years, were the barriers which impriſoned the manufactures of our iſland at once removed. Great was the exultation, and confident the hopes of the people upon this memorable occaſion. An immediate influx of wealth, an inſtantaneous improvement of circumſtances, were predicted and expected. Manufactures were to have ſtarted into vigour in every corner of the iſland, and the magic of the words *Free Trade* were, like the ſpells of an enchantreſs, to have diſſipated in a moment the enervating effects of a century's debility and diſeaſe. The confidence of hope was more than equalled by the mortification of diſappointment. The Iriſh felt not immediately the predicted alteration of circumſtances; their manufactures were neither viſibly extended nor conſiderably improved. The ſources of this deficiency were not now ſo obvious as before. It is our buſineſs to inveſtigate the cauſes which have prevented the ſpeedy realization of ſuch ſanguine expectations.

These

These appear neither obscure or extraordinary. Manufactures are necessarily plants of slow growth in the most favourable situations. Even where capital is abundant, and a habit of industry established, it requires time, perseverance, and encouragement to advance them to any considerable degree of perfection. The circumstances of Ireland in the year 1779, instead of favourable, were adverse to the establishment and improvement of any considerable manufactures. The various oppressions we have already detailed left us, in a considerable degree, destitute of capital, a foundation so absolutely necessary to any institutions of this nature. From causes already explained, an equally essential requisite, the habit of industry, was almost unknown. Skill we possessed little of; and experience we had none. These various preliminary necessaries were not in any country to be instantaneously obtained; and, as was before observed, even where a nation is possessed of them, novel manufactures are gradual in their approaches to perfection. How then could any well-grounded expectations of an exception to so general a rule be rationally formed in Ireland, a country destitute

tute of every ſuch advantage? The cool and deliberate reaſoner, who conſulted the experience of ages, and conſidered the nature of the improvements alluded to, would have looked forward to a gradual, not confidently expected an inſtantaneous eſtabliſhment of flouriſhing manufactures. The period which has elapſed ſince the emancipation of our iſland has confirmed the juſtice of ſuch a concluſion. Manufactures have been introduced; their improvement has been ſlow, but they are ſilently, gradually, and ſteadily advancing to the deſired acmé of perfection: theſe advances will be daily more conſiderable, and, like the motion of a body deſcending to the earth, acquire an accelerated velocity as they approach the point of deſtination.

But what are the meaſures moſt adviſeable to be purſued for encouraging and extending the manufactures we have eſtabliſhed? Let us examine thoſe which have with ſuch intent been adopted by other nations, and determine which are applicable or inapplicable to our ſituation.

The expedients which nations have had recourſe to, for encouraging and extending their manufactures,

manufactures, may be arranged under the following heads—1. Permitting a free and unrestrained exportation of goods manufactured. 2. *Encouraging* this exportation by bounties. 3. Prohibiting the importation of any such manufactures from other countries. 4. Prohibiting the exportation of the primum of which they are composed. And, 5. Prohibiting the exportation of that primum in any stage of manufacture short of the last. These we shall consider in order.

The necessity of a free exportation to the encouragement of manufactures we have already noticed; it has been universally acknowledged, and such exportation has been permitted in every country where the advancement of manufactures engages the smallest concern of the government. Since the settlement of 1779, Ireland enjoys a free exportation for all her manufactures to every market in Europe, Africa, and the New World, as far as the respective institutions of the different nations admit. From any export to the East Indies she is cut off, by the compliance of her own legislature with the wishes of England; nor does a distant and very expensive commerce of this nature appear, it must be confessed, well suited to her preſent ſtate of capital †. The regulations of many ſtates prevent the free importation of the foreign manufactures of all countries in order to encourage their own. Theſe we muſt unavoidably ſubmit to, unleſs ſome expedient can be deviſed to perſuade them to open their markets to us. From none are we ſo completely excluded by inſtitutions of this nature as from thoſe of Great Britain, in almoſt every article except that of linen; while our markets are laid open to every manufacture of theirs. Whether any ſteps can be with prudence taken to exclude them from our markets, or to effect an equal liberty of import and export between both kingdoms, we ſhall hereafter inquire.

A free and unlimited exportation has not been deemed ſufficient to encourage manufactures. Government in different countries have been in the practice of granting bounties on the exportation of manufactured produce; and thereby attracting a greater number of hands to particular branches

† By an act paſſed this laſt ſeſſion Ireland is admitted to a participation of the monopoly of the Eaſt India Company.

branches of induſtry than they would naturally have engaged, and enabling them to ſell their manufactures at a cheaper rate in foreign markets than they could otherwiſe afford. The linen manufacture is almoſt the only one which has obtained the encouragement of a bounty on exportation in Ireland, and that at a very conſiderable annual expence to the nation.

The utility of all bounties has been arraigned by Doctor Smith. We have attempted to ſhew, that that on the exportation of corn is, for particular reaſons, advantageous to Ireland. His objections to bounties on manufactures appear much more applicable to our ſituation, and ſcarcely liable to refutation. " Bounties upon " the exportation of any home-made commodity " are liable firſt to that general objection which " may be made to all expedients of the mercan- " tile ſyſtem, the objection of forcing ſome part " of the induſtry of a country into a channel " *leſs* advantageous than that in which it would " run of its own accord; and, ſecondly, to the " particular objection of forcing it, not only into " a channel that is leſs advantageous, but into

" one

" one which is actually *disadvantageous*; the " trade which *cannot* be carried on but by means " of a bounty, being *necessarily a losing* trade." For " bounties, it is allowed, ought to be given " to those branches of trade *only* which cannot " be carried on without them. But every branch " of trade in which the merchant can sell his " goods for a price which replaces to him, with " the ordinary profits of stock, the whole capital " employed in preparing and sending them to " market, *can* be carried on without a bounty. " Those trades only require bounties in which " the merchant is obliged to sell his goods for " a price which does not replace to him his ca- " pital, together with the ordinary profit, or in " which he is obliged to sell them for less than " it really costs him to send them to market. " Such a trade, therefore, necessarily eats up in " every operation a part of the capital employed " in it; and is of such a nature, that if all other " trades resembled it, there would soon be no " capital left in the country."

The principles here advanced are perfectly clear. If a manufacture can be carried on with-

out

out the aid of bounty, no bounty ſhould be granted. If it cannot be carried on without ſuch aſſiſtance, it is neceſſarily a loſing buſineſs, and ſhould not be encouraged. It diminiſhes, inſtead of augmenting, the general capital and ſtock of ſociety, the general fund for the employment of its people. The augmentation of that capital ſhould be the principal end and aim of the people of Ireland; and would be the moſt certain and effectual mode of eſtabliſhing and extending manufactures among them. The legiſlature, therefore, ſhould withſtand all attempts to obtain new bounties on the exportation of manufactures, or at leaſt grant them to infant eſtabliſhments of this nature with extreme caution. Such attempts will certainly be made, and if any are to be granted, let them be taken from the very conſiderable ſum which has been ſo long deſtined for the linen manufacture only. It would not, perhaps, be adviſeable *at once* to deprive the linen manufacture of this encouragement; but, I think, a great part may with perfect ſafety be gradually withdrawn, and applied to more uſeful and neceſſary purpoſes.

The

The encouragement which manufacturers are always moſt clamorous to obtain, and which they have in general been moſt ſucceſsful in obtaining, is the monopoly of the home-market of the country in which they are eſtabliſhed. This is ſecured to them by loading with high duties, or abſolutely prohibiting, the importation of ſuch goods from foreign countries as they are engaged in manufacturing. Many ſtrong, and ſometimes outrageous attempts have been made in Ireland to obtain a ſimilar monopoly, by what were termed *Protecting Duties*, but hitherto without effect. The influence of the Engliſh government in our councils has, perhaps, tended not a little to prevent ſuch requiſitions from being granted.

The propriety and utility of granting a monopoly of the home-market to the manufacturers of *any* country, by loading with heavy duties, or abſolutely prohibiting, importation from abroad, has, in a former part of this Eſſay, been already pretty fully diſcuſſed, (ſee page 106.) And from conſidering the general tendency of the opinions there advanced, it will appear pretty evident, that the importance of the relative intereſts of a peo-

ple

ple at large, and of a few interefted manufacturers, are to be weighed and appreciated, before any fuch reftraints can with propriety be impofed. The obfervations alluded to have, in a great meafure, anticipated any which could be offered at prefent; and the objections ftated to the adoption of fuch a plan, under any circumftances, feem peculiarly applicable to the Irifh people. By recurring to the paffage quoted, it will be found that the direct tendency of all regulations of this nature is, to diminifh the general capital of a nation in proportion to the difference of the annual amount between the price of the domeftic and foreign manufactures in queftion. Deficiency of capital, however, is the principal obftruction to the eftablifhment and improvement of manufactures, and every other fource of employment in Ireland. Thofe regulations, therefore, which directly tend to the diminution of that capital, cannot be the beft calculated to eftablifh and extend them. Want of fkill is another caufe of the unimproved ftate of our different fabrics; but the regulations in queftion would not, in our opinion, produce in Ireland the fecondary advantage of augmenting that ſkill, or of improving the texture and value, and conſequently increaſing the exportation of the manufacture ſo favoured. The manufacturers of our iſland, it is to be lamented, poſſeſs no very great ſhare of that ſpirit of emulation which conduces ſo much to the perfection of any fabric. The monopoly of the home-market being ſecured would neceſſarily prevent any competition, and would deaden whatever portion of emulation they are actuated by; and as the inhabitants of the country muſt neceſſarily buy whatever the manufacturers offer for ſale, and at whatever price they pleaſe to impoſe on it, their reſpective fabrics, until ſome competition ariſe among themſelves, would probably be leſs valuable than even at preſent, and their ſale in foreign markets be conſequently either diminiſhed or annihilated.

The advantage of diſpoſing of his goods without any expence of freight, commiſſion, inſurance, duties, and a variety of other charges, is ſo conſiderable, that it will always ſecure the home market to the domeſtic, againſt the foreign manufacturer, if there be any approach to equality in the reſpective value of their ſeveral

fabrics.

fabrics. The only country permitted to dispute the home-market with the Irish manufacturer is Great Britain. Almost all manufactured produce imported thence into this country is subject to low duties, and the different articles are, besides, liable to the expence of carriage from the manufactories to the sea-port towns, and of freight, insurance, commission, port-duties, &c. from thence into Ireland. The duties vary on different articles. The following table of some of them will shew that the home-market is, to no inconsiderable degree, already secured to the Irish manufacturer.

	From Great Britain.		
	£.	s.	d.
Beer, per barrel, 32 gallons -	—	4	3 9/20
Bottles, per dozen - -	—	—	3 6/10
Buttons, per cent. - -	10	10	—
Cotton manufactures, per cent. -	10	10	—
Callicoes, per yard - ..	—	1	— 3/5
Drapery, new, per yard -	—	—	2 1/10
———, old, per yard -	—	—	6 5/10
Earthenware, per cent. - -	15	15	—

Hardware

	£.	s.	d.
Hardware, the duties vary on the different articles.			
Lawns, ornamented, per cent. -	10	10	—
Muslin, foreign, per yard - -	—	1	11 1/10
British, per yard - -	—	—	10½
Paper, post, per cent. - -	10	10	—
Plated goods, per cent. - -	10	10	—
Stockings, cotton or thread, per cent. - - - -	10	10	—
———, worsted, per pair -	—	—	7 10/50

To these duties are to be added the expence of freight, commission, insurance, and port-duties, which vary in amount, according to the different weight and bulk of the articles imported; on cottons and woollens, these amount to about two or three per cent.; on beer about eighteen per cent.; on hardware about fifteen per cent.

If, with these advantages in his favour, the Irish domestic manufacturer cannot support a competition in the home-market, it certainly would be unjust to oblige the people at large, by prohibitory duties, to purchase their goods ſor any price which they may pleaſe to impoſe on them, although ſo much inferior in value. This would both diminiſh the general capital, and, for reaſons already aſſigned, it would not, at leaſt for a long ſeries of years, and until ſome competition took place among the manufacturers, increaſe their dexterity and ſkill, or the degree of perfection in their fabrics. Want of capital, and want of ſkill, are the two principal deficiencies we labour under. Regulations of this nature, inſtead of increaſing, would diminiſh both. When our capital and ſkill have advanced higher in the ſcale of perfection, and they are advancing every day, the duties and expences to which foreign goods are liable will effectually ſecure the home market to our manufacturers. At the period when the Commercial Propoſitions were agitated, and it was in contemplation to lower duties paid on Iriſh manufactures imported into Great Britain, to the rates impoſed on Britiſh imported into Ireland, the manufacturers of England, whoſe jealouſy is ſo apt on the ſlighteſt foundation to take the alarm, were ſatisfied that ſuch duties, and the expence of freight, commiſſion, &c. would effectually ſecure the home

market

market to them. The following is the report of the Lords of the Committee of Council: "The
" duties imposed by this plan on woollen goods
" imported from Ireland will be lower than those
" on any other article of Irish growth or manu-
" facture, being about six-pence per yard on old
" drapery, and two-pence on new, which is, on
" an average, not more than five per cent.; and
" yet the merchants and manufacturers in this
" branch of commerce, whom the committee
" have examined, appear by their evidence to
" have very little apprehension of a competition.
" The duties on the importation of all other
" goods, the growth and manufacture of Ireland,
" into this kingdom, will, according to the pro-
" posed plan, be at least ten per cent. and on
" some articles considerably more; which, with
" the charges of freight, insurance, commission,
" and port-charges, will, in the judgment of the
" Committee, be amply sufficient to secure a due
" preference to the subjects of Great Britain in
" their own market."

Another circumstance which must render the adoption of any regulations under the denomination of Protecting Duties, which would ſecure the monopoly of the home market to Iriſh manufacturers, particularly detrimental to Ireland, is, that by raiſing the profits of manufacturing occupations much higher than thoſe of agricultural, it would neceſſarily draw from the latter buſineſs, which is ſo much more advantageous to ſociety, a portion of that capital which would otherwiſe be employed in it. Agriculture, however, for the many reaſons already ſtated, is the occupation which ſhould be peculiarly encouraged in Ireland, and any regulations or reſtrictions which, even remotely, tend to diſcourage or depreſs it, will be proportionably detrimental to the intereſt and employment of the people at large.

Of the two caſes ſtated by Smith, in which it would be advantageous for a nation to lay reſtraints upon the produce of foreign, in favour of domeſtic induſtry (ſee above, Part I. page 113,) neither are applicable to the preſent ſituation of Ireland; no argument can be deduced from them, under our circumſtances, in favour of protecting duties or prohibitions. There is another caſe ſtated by Smith, in which he ſays

it

it may be matter of deliberation, whether a nation ſhould impoſe high duties on foreign manufactured produce or not, and that is, when a nation reſtrains, by high duties or prohibitions, the importation of the ſame manufactures into their ports. The importation of almoſt all Iriſh manufactures into Great Britain, linen only excepted, is either prohibited or reſtrained by high duties; and it may, therefore, be deemed eligible to impoſe the ſame reſtraints upon Britiſh manufactures, which they impoſe upon ours. "There "may be good policy," ſays Smith, "in retaliations of this kind, when there is a probability that they will procure a repeal of the "high duties or prohibitions complained of: "the recovery of a great foreign market will "generally more than compenſate the tranſitory "inconvenience of paying dearer during a ſhort "time for ſome ſort of goods. But when there "is no probability that any ſuch repeal can be "procured, it ſeems a bad method of compenſating the injury done to ſome claſſes of our "people, to do another injury ourſelves, not "only to theſe claſſes, but to almoſt all the "other claſſes of them." This is preciſely the

caſe

caſe of Ireland. The Engliſh would never be prevailed upon to open their markets to our manufactures by meaſures of this nature. On the contrary, ſuch a war of prohibitions would, it is probable, both cloſe their barriers more firmly againſt us, and ultimately exclude us from the Britiſh market for our linens, at preſent the moſt valuable of any we are in poſſeſſion of.

For the many reaſons advanced, therefore, the protecting duties, ſo loudly clamoured for at different periods, ſhould never be given to Iriſh manufactures. Thoſe who demand them are actuated by ſhort-ſighted and merely intereſted motives. Thoſe who ſupport them from patriotic principles are guilty of an error in judgment, and cannot poſſibly have ſtudied the ſubject in the minute manner, and with the extenſive views, it neceſſarily requires. The advantages our manufactures poſſeſs in the home-market are already ſufficiently great; if, with theſe advantages, they are not able to diſpute the market with foreigners, the manufactures deſerve not greater partiality, nor the manufacturers greater attention.

The loading with heavy duties, or totally prohibiting, the exportation of the primum of manufactures, has been another device adopted for their encouragement. By preventing any competition of foreigners, reſtraints of this nature infallibly ſecure ſuch materials at a cheaper rate to manufacturers than they could obtain them if a free and fair competition were allowed. The only primum, of which we naturally poſſeſs any conſiderable quantity, is wool. In order to favour the woollen manufactures of England, the export of wool from Ireland to any country but Great Britain has been long prohibited. Would it be an adviſeable meaſure to prohibit its exportation to *any* country, in order to ſecure it at a cheaper rate to our own manufacturers? The policy of Great Britain, in prohibiting the exportation of wool, has been by many writers keenly diſputed. It has been aſſerted, that its very low price in the home-market * has rendered the grower ſo careleſs as to its quality, that the fineneſs and value of the wool have progreſſively

* The average price of wool in England is 6d. per pound; in Ireland 10½d.; in France 17d.

fively decreafed, that even the quantity is diminifhed, and that in confequence of fuch neglect, the manufacturers have for a long time been obliged to import Spanifh wool, of which all the finer manufactures are now entirely compofed. (See Anderfon on National Induftry, Letter XII.) Thefe fuppofed evil confequences, however, of prohibiting the exportation of wool, have been difputed by many refpectable writers on the fubject. Doctor Smith affigns very fatisfactory reafons for concluding, that the prohibition cannot have produced thefe effects. "It may be "thought," fays he, "that the reduction of the "price of wool, by difcouraging the growing of "wool, muft have reduced its annual produce. "I am difpofed to believe, however, that this is "not the cafe. The growing of wool is not the "chief purpofe for which the fheep farmer em"ploys his induftry and ftock; he expects his "profit, not fo much from the fleece as from the "carcafe; and the average price of the latter "muft make up to him any deficiency in the "average price of the former. The degradation "in the price of wool, therefore, is not likely, "in an improved and cultivated country, to oc"cafion

" cafion any diminution in the annual produce " of that commodity. Its effects, however, up- " on its quality, may be perhaps thought very " great. It happens, however, that the goodnefs " of the fleece depends, in a great meafure, upon " the health, growth, and bulk of the animal. " The fame attention which is neceffary for the " improvement of the carcafe, is, in fome re- " fpects, fufficient for that of the fleece. Not- " withftanding the degradation of price, Eng- " lifh wool is faid to have improved confi- " derably during the courfe even of the pre- " fent century †."

If the prohibition againft the export of wool, from the peculiarity in the mode of its produce, be a meafure not injurious in England, its adoption muft be much more adviseable in Ireland. The prevalence of grazing we have fhewn to be moft deftructive in its operation. Many of the moft fertile tracts in the kingdom, and the beft fitted for agriculture, are ftill covered with fheep. Any meafure, therefore, not otherwife difadvantageous,

† *Abridged* from Book IV. Ch. VIII. of the Wealth of Nations.

tageous, which diminiſhes the profits of this ſpecies of grazing, and tends to confine ſheep to thoſe diſtricts naturally adapted to their rearing and fattening, and incapable of being ſubmitted to the more uſeful culture of the plough, ought to be adopted without heſitation. Such reſtrictions, beſides, by lowering the price of wool, aſſiſt our woollen manufacturers; they encourage an uſeful ſpecies of induſtry and employment, and diſcourage a buſineſs which affords no employment at all. Should, therefore, the exportation of wool to Great Britain be prohibited? Such a meaſure is unneceſſary. The exportation has ſpontaneouſly, almoſt, ceaſed, and that for reaſons we ſhall proceed to ſtate. Wool ſells in Ireland, on an average, at tenpence-halfpenny per pound, in England at ſixpence, and the general quality of the former is inferior to that of the latter. (See the Report of the Committee of Council in England on the Iriſh Propoſitions.) A licenſe for exportation from the Lord Lieutenant is alſo neceſſary, the coſt of which amounts to about fourpence-halfpenny per ſtone. If we add to this the charges of freight, commiſſion, inſurance, &c. it will not be ſurpriſing that the

export

export of wool to England has been almost entirely abandoned. It was at one period exported to Great Britain in very large quantities. In the year 1698 the English manufacturers petitioned that the importation of woollen and worsted yarn from Ireland should be prohibited. To please the English monopolist, as usual, heavy duties were accordingly laid on its exportation from this island. The Irish were, consequently, necessitated to export their wool to England in its natural state. This they did in large quantities. The export of wool to England in 1698 was 377,520 stone. In the year 1739 the English manufacturers petitioned that the restraints imposed according to their desire in 1698, on the exportation of Irish yarn, should be removed; their petition was of course complied with, and this gave a considerable check to the export of wool to England. It has since that period progressively declined, and is at present very trifling. At an average of seven years, ending 1770, the annual export of wool to England was but 18976 stone. At an average of seven years, ending 1777, it was but 1415 stone. It has since that period decreased still more, and is at present scarcely

ſcarcely worthy notice. This diminution has been occaſioned, partly by the increaſed price of wool in Ireland; an increaſe proceeding from our peaſantry being more numerous, and better clothed, than formerly, and almoſt entirely with domeſtic manufacture, which neceſſarily increaſed the demand, and conſequently the price of wool. The riſe of price in wool has alſo been partly occaſioned from its being ſmuggled to France, though I believe this trade at preſent very trifling; but the price has been principally, I believe, augmented by the exportation of wool manufactured into yarn into England. The expediency of permitting the exportation of this yarn we ſhall next examine; it is the principal object of conſideration in the ſubſequent article of our inquiry.

The laſt expedient we ſhall conſider which has been deviſed and practiſed for the encouragement of manufactures, is, prohibiting the exportation of any primum in any ſtage of manufacture ſhort of the laſt.

This has been another favourite object with the manufacturers of different countries. Not satisfied with obtaining a monopoly of the home-market against all buyers of their manufactures, by excluding any but their own, they have endeavoured, and in general too successfully, to obtain a similar monopoly against all sellers of any of the materials employed in these manufactures, by preventing any purchaser from coming in competition with themselves. Thus, by contriving to buy as cheap and sell as dear as possible, they endeavour to augment their own profits to the utmost, at the expence of every other order in the state; and persuade you, that this is the speediest and most infallible method of enriching a nation.

The two great articles of Irish produce, which come under this head of our inquiry, are, Linen and woollen yarn; the former of which is employed in large quantities in cotton, as well as linen manufactures, and the latter in different branches of the woollen manufacture. Linen yarn is liable, on exportation, to a duty of five shillings per hundred weight; woollen yarn is

exported

exported duty free. Would it or would it not be advantageous to impoſe high duties on, or totally prohibit the exportation of theſe materials, in order to encourage our manufactures? The effects of ſuch a meaſure would infallibly be, to throw the very great numbers at preſent employed in Ireland in ſpinning linen and woollen yarn entirely on the mercy of the linen, cotton, and woollen manufacturers. Freed from the competition of any other purchaſers, the manufacturers would regulate the price of theſe articles themſelves, and infallibly give only the loweſt which the ſpinners could afford to receive. In any country this would be unjuſt and impolitic; in Ireland it would be peculiarly ſo. The lower claſs of people are thoſe whom it ſhould be the peculiar object of the legiſlature to relieve and enrich. Numbers are employed in the manufacturing of linen and woollen yarn, who could ſcarcely find employment in any other line. To throw them upon the generoſity of a claſs of people who have, in every ſituation, evinced the moſt ſelfiſh and monopoliſing ſpirit, would be a moſt effectual mode to diminiſh the amount of their ſcanty earnings, and to leſſen a principal

ſource

ſource of their employment. The demands of the manufacturers, on this head, are truly unjuſtifiable. It is abſurd to ſuppoſe that the export of a manufacture, becauſe it has not arr'ved at the laſt ſtage of perfection, cannot be ſerviceable to a country; and it is a falſehood to aſſert that the manufacturers of Ireland do not already poſſeſs a ſufficient advantage, in the purchaſe of thoſe articles, over the manufacturers of other nations. The Engliſh manufacturer purchaſes thoſe ſame articles at a much higher price than the Iriſh; converts them into complete fabrics, and afterwards underſells the Iriſhman in his own market. This will appear from a very ſhort calculation. Iriſh linen yarn pays a duty of five ſhillings per hundred weight on exportation; which, at the rate of ſix pounds ſterling per hundred weight, the average price of linen yarn, is four one-fifth per cent. in the purchaſe: the charges of freight, commiſſion, inſurance, &c. as depoſed before the Committee of Council, are five per cent. The Engliſh, therefore, purchaſe our linen yarn at nine one-fifth per cent. advance, beſide the difference of price in the two countries. The diſadvantage at which the Engliſh manufacturer

purchaſes

purchafes our woollen yarn, in confequence of the expence of licenfe, port-duties, freight, commiffion, &c. is ftated in the evidence given before the Committee of Council to be about fixpence-halfpenny per cent.

With thefe advantages, however, in the purchafe of the materials of their fabrics, the Irifh linen, cotton, and woollen manufacturers are not fatisfied. They would have us deprefs the induftry, diminifh the earnings, and curtail the employment of thoufands of the poor, in order to give them an advantage over the Englifh manufacturer, befide thofe they already enjoy, which are fo very confiderable.

We may form an adequate idea of the importance of the manufacture of linen yarn to the employment and emolument of the poor, from what Doctor Smith has advanced on a fimilar fubject in England. "In the different opera-"tions," fays he, "which are neceffary for the "preparation of linen yarn, a good deal more "induftry is employed than in the fubfequent "operation of preparing linen cloth from linen "yarn.

" yarn. To ſay nothing of the induſtry of the " flax-growers and flax-dreſſers, three or four " ſpinners at leaſt are neceſſary to keep one " weaver in conſtant employment; and more " than four-fifths of the whole quantity of la- " bour, neceſſary for the preparation of linen " cloth, is employed in that of linen yarn.— " But it is the induſtry which is carried on for " the benefit of the rich and the powerful that " is principally encouraged by our mercantile " ſyſtem. That which is carried on for the be- " nefit of the poor and the indigent is too often " either neglected or oppreſſed." The importance of the manufacture of linen yarn will be, from theſe obſervations, abundantly evident. The importance of that of woollen yarn will appear from the ſubſequent calculation.

Mr. Young, in his inquiries reſpecting the manufacture of this article, diſcovered the following particulars. (See his Tour, p. 252.)

	£.	*s.*	*d.*
The coſt of 5000 ſtone of wool, at 16s. per ſtone, was - -	4000	—	—

	£. s. d.	£. s. d.
Combing this wool was - -	520 — —	
Spinning it - -	1560 — —	
		2080 — —
Value of the yarn - -		6080 — —

The mere labour, therefore, in the manufacturing this yarn was better than one-third of its whole value. Another calculation, he makes elsewhere, gives somewhat the same result. " *Bay* " *yarn.* A woman, on an average, spins three " skains a-day, which weigh a quarter of a " pound; the value spun is from ten-pence to a " shilling, medium ten-pence three farthings.

	£. s. d.
" Combing it - - -	— — 1
" Spinning - - -	— — 2½
	— — 3½
" Value of wool - -	— — 7¼
" Value of yarn - -	— — 10¾"

The

The proportion of the labour employed in its manufacture, to that of the value of the yarn, is pretty much the ſame as in the former calculation, about one-third.

The average annual value of woollen yarn exported from Ireland is 350,000l. ſterling; of this ſum one-third, or about 116,666l. ſterling is to be ſet down to mere labour, and is, therefore, annually diſtributed in the employment of the loweſt claſs; a circumſtance of conſiderable conſequence, where the earnings of that claſs are ſo ſcanty, and their poverty ſo conſiderable, as in Ireland.

As the Iriſh manufacturer, therefore, already enjoys a conſiderable advantage, in the purchaſe of linen and woollen yarn, over every manufacturing competitor; as, by the export of thoſe articles, employment is afforded to thouſands of the lower claſs, who could not otherwiſe well obtain it; as the employment and aggrandizement of that claſs are, in Ireland, objects which ſhould claim peculiar attention and regard, any duties on, or prohibition againſt, the exportation of linen or woollen yarn, can only be calculated to give a prejudicial monopoly to a few interested manufacturers, whose advantages are already sufficiently great; and to depress the industry and obstruct the employment of a class of people, more numerous, more indigent, and more in need of assistance and support.

Another expedient, which has been recommended for promoting the manufactures of Ireland, and consequently the employment of her people, is, lowering the legal rate of interest. The many advantages which a nation derives from the fixed rate of interest being a low one, have been so fully explained by Sir Jos. Child, and his work is in such general circulation, that any recapitulation of the observations and arguments he adduced would be superfluous. An attempt was lately made to lower the rate of interest in this country to five per cent. and the subject was at that time very fully discussed. The only argument of any weight adduced in opposition to a measure so beneficial, was, that a considerable portion of the stock and capital of the kingdom was English; that the only temptation

tion the proprietors had to lay it out in this country was the additional intereſt which was paid here, and that if that were reduced, the greater part of it would be withdrawn. This argument, however, is completely refuted by advertiſements which every day appear, offering Engliſh money at intereſt on good ſecurities at five per cent. Many ſums are actually borrowed at preſent at that rate; and it certainly would conſiderably aſſiſt the manufacturer and trader to have the legal intereſt reduced to that ſtandard; for as long as it is fixed at ſix per cent. the majority of money-lenders will expect and receive that ſum, notwithſtanding any partial exceptions of money lent at five or lower.

Such are the different expedients which have been practiſed for introducing, encouraging, and extending manufactures, in different parts of Europe; and ſo little, in our opinion, is the applicability of the majority of them to the manufactures of Ireland in her preſent ſtate. Will you, therefore, give no extraordinary encouragement to the manufactures of your country? If a manufacturer aſked ſuch a queſtion, I would anſwer him

him thus: You aſk for encouragement; the occupation you purſue is one of conſiderable conſequence to ſociety, and if I could grant the encouragement and privileges you deſire, without injuring, by ſuch conceſſion, the ſtill more important intereſts of the remaining very great majority of the people, I ſhould willingly acquieſce in your requiſition; but the promotion of thoſe intereſts, and the privileges you labour to obtain, are perfectly incompatible. The advantages you are already in poſſeſſion of are far from inconſiderable: by the ſettlement of 1779, the markets of the greater part of the commercial world were thrown open to you; duties are already impoſed upon different articles of manufactured produce, which, although not amounting to prohibitions, are ſufficient, with the unavoidable charges of freight and other expences, to give you a decided advantage in your home-market, and are as heavy as can be impoſed with any degree of prudence, or ſufficient conſideration for the intereſts of ſociety at large. Similar duties, ſimilar expences, and the cheapneſs of labour, afford you equal advantages in the purchaſe of different neceſſary articles in the lower ſtages

ſtages of your reſpective fabrics: if, ſituated thus, you are unable to meet, with all his diſadvantages, the foreign manufacturer in your home, or to diſpute with him the preference in foreign markets, I muſt impute your deficiency to want of capital and want of ſkill, and I cannot think that the one would be augmented, or the other improved, by the meaſures you are ſo very deſirous ſhould be adopted. The reſtraints you laboured under before 1779 deprived you of ſkill, and your nation of capital. The removal of thoſe reſtraints, although it laid open to you the opportunity of improving in both, could not inſtantaneouſly inveſt you with an adequate portion of either. Such important acquiſitions muſt be gradually obtained; you are gradually obtaining them, and your manufactures are in a ſtate of ſteady and progreſſive increaſe. Perſevere in the ſame plan; let induſtry preſide over your labours; let emulation animate your attention and ingenuity; and you will ſpeedily not only ſecure the home-market for your fabrics againſt all rivals, but diſpute with them a preference in the foreign.

Conformably to these sentiments, the minute inquirer will find that the different manufactures of Ireland are daily improving and extending. Of this the following facts will afford very convincing proofs. Several of the tables I have not been able to bring down to the present day, and must plead the same excuse, and indulge the same expectations, as on a former similar occasion.

Woollen manufacture. This is extending and improving considerably, especially in the coarser fabrics. An infinitely greater proportion of the home-demand is supplied by them than before the extension of our trade in 1779; and it may reasonably be expected that our manufacturers will, in those branches, soon exclude all foreign competitors.

The increase of our exports in the woollen branch, since the removal of our commercial restraints, will be seen from the following table, a continuation of which I have not yet been able to procure.

Export.		Drapery, New.	Drapery, Old.
		Yards.	Yards.
Years ending March	1780	8653	494
	1781	286859	3740
	1782	336607½	4633
	1783	538061	40589

The

The progreſſive increaſe of our woollen may be judged from that of the total of our exports, which I have obtained down to 1787.

		£.	s.	d.
This was in 1783	-	2935707	17	6¼
1784	-	3326211	16	6
1785	-	3737068	—	7½
1786	-	3957396	18	11½
1787	-	4238345	13	11¾

Cotton Manufacture. This is daily increaſing and improving, and proportionately engroſſing the home-market, but particularly in the fuſtian and muſlin line. Some information reſpecting the increaſing ſtate of this trade may be received from the following tables.

Export of fuſtians from Ireland to America was in

1781	-	1108 yards.
1782	-	None.
1783	-	24296
1784	-	47237

Export

Export of cotton and mixed goods from Ireland to America was in

		£.	s.	d.	
1781	-	145	12	4	value.
1782	-	414	7	6	
1783	-	1148	16	—	
1784	-	8319	18	2	

The importation of the materials, cotton wool and cotton yarn, has increafed in the following proportion:

		Cotton Wool. Cwt.	Cotton Yarn. Cwt.
Average of three years ending -	1773	2550	2226
	1783	3236	5405
	1787	7153	21615

Glafs manufacture. In the bottle line this is increafing. In the finer branches the Waterford manufactory has improved and extended itfelf to an aftonifhing degree. It fupplies at prefent the greater part of the home-market of the kingdom; this is univerfally known; it may be proved from

from the confiderable decreafe in the importation of one article, drinking glaffes. The average number imported for

Three years ending	1773	was	209222
Ditto - -	1783	—	22248
Ditto - -	1787	—	4648

Our firft export of glafs was in 1781, fince which time it has progreffively increafed.

Paper manufacture. The improvements in this branch are well known. Its fales in the home-market are proportionately increafing, and it bids fair in a fhort fpace of time to fupply it almoft entirely.

Silk manufacture. From our want of the primum; from the variation in fancy as to the different articles of this fabric, which we muft always copy from London; and from various other caufes, this manufacture is flower in its progrefs to perfection than any other; nor is this to be much lamented. The difadvantages it muft labour under will always confiderably impede its progrefs; and the other branches of manufactures

tures will, for a length of time, afford ſufficient employment to the hands, which could derive occupation in this. Still, however, it is improving; damaſks, luſtrings, and handkerchiefs, of a very good quality, are produced by our artiſts. But their particular excellence is in mixed goods, as tabinets and poplins; thoſe have been long celebrated, and the home-market for them is entirely ſupplied by domeſtic artiſts. It is with pleaſure I obſerve they are forcing their way into foreign markets. Some entries of them have been lately made for Holland.

On the whole, it may with pleaſure be remarked, that our manufactures, as well in the branches particulariſed as in others more ſubordinate, are daily and ſteadily increaſing. This is in itſelf another proof that our backwardneſs in them has not been owing, ſince 1779, to any impolitic reſtrictions, or to the home-market's not being ſufficiently protected, but to want of capital and want of ſkill, two material defects which could not be immediately obviated, but which are daily and rapidly diminiſhing. From

a perſeverance

a perſeverance in the ſame line of conduct, therefore, and from a rejection of any impolitic duties or prohibitions, may juſtly be expected a progreſſive and conſiderable extenſion and improvement in all our manufactures, and a conſequent proportionate increaſe in the employment of our people.

Since concluding and ſending the preceding ſheets to the preſs, I have, through the medium of Sir Hercules Langriſhe, obtained the ſubſequent continuation of the tables of Export and Import—his promptitude and politeneſs in procuring the neceſſary information, demand my peculiar acknowledgments. The reſult turns out highly favourable to the concluſions attempted to be eſtabliſhed in the foregoing pages.

An Account of the following Articles exported from and imported into Ireland for ten Years, ending 25th March 1792, and of the total Value of Exports during the same Period.

Years ending 25th March	Articles of Exportation.						Articles of Importation.	
	Drapery.		Yarn.		Cotton and linen mixed manufacture.	Value of the Exports.	Wool, Cotton.	Yarn, Cotton.
	New.	Old.	Woollen.	Worsted.				
	Yards.	Yards.	Stones.	Stones.	Value.	Value.	Cwt.	Pounds.
					£.	£.		
1783	538061	40589	440	66677	1418	2907922	4550	6516
1784	666298	35329	97	100563	9548	3326211	53	547
1785	770032	34250	490	94729	9382	3737068	5223	4711
1786	349628	10435	803	74931	4443	3956736	7260	22188
1787	206849	15329	—	54862	5216	4238333	8977	37945
1788	315111	7747	31884	7109	7545	4361664	10728	45015
1789	363196	7833	—	26316	4616	4103339	13516	83814
1790	352022	8312	—	39973	14522	4826360	11911	77687
1791	320491	15085	—	38064	9628	4863658	14649	205515
1792	384396	18669	—	53644	16988	5321358	10233	298351

This

This table affords many proofs that the manufactures of this kingdom are in a ſtate of progreſſive increaſe, unaſſiſted by the different prohibitory duties which we have in the preceding ſection reprobated as unneceſſary, nay prejudicial. The three firſt years, indeed, are remarkable for the exportation of an unuſual number of yards of new and old drapery; but this ſeems to have been owing to the great ſpeculation excited at that period, by the pacification of America, the market of which became in conſequence ſoon overſtocked. Since the current of exportation has ſubſided into its natural channel theſe manufactures are gaining ground, and their home-conſumption has advanced much more rapidly than their exportation. But many other favourable concluſions may be drawn from the tables in queſtion.

1. Although the manufacture of woollen and worſted yarn has not diminiſhed in the kingdom, the exportation of theſe articles has been conſiſiderably leſſened. The average annual amount of the exportation for five years, ending 1787,

was

was in round numbers 78718 ſtones. A ſimilar average, ending 1792, is only 39398 ſtones. As the exportation has not been loaded with any duty, this diminution can only be aſcribed to the extenſion of the woollen manufacture within the kingdom.

2. The exportation of cotton and linen mixed goods has been increaſing. The annual average of the value of ſuch goods exported for five years, ending 1787, is 6001l. A ſimilar average, ending 1792, is 10659l. But,

3. The manufacture and home-conſumption of cotton manufactures have increaſed in a much greater proportion, as appears from the great increaſe in the importation of the raw materials, cotton wool and cotton yarn. The average annual importation of theſe articles during the two before-mentioned periods ſtands thus:

Average of five years importation of cotton wool, ending 1787, is -	5212 Cwt.
Ditto, ending 1792, - -	12207

Average

Average of five years importation of cotton yarn, ending 1787, is -	14281 lbs.
Ditto, ending 1792, - -	142076

4. The total amount of our exports has confiderably increafed.

	£.
The average annual amount of five years, ending 1787, is - -	3633234
Ditto, ending 1792, - -	4695275

§ III. Commerce.

This division necessarily brief—Carrying trade does not afford much employment—or much profit—A monopoly of it, therefore, by the people of Ireland would be injurious—The object of commercial regulations should be chiefly our admission to foreign ports—Intercourse between Ireland and Great Britain—Origin of the British prohibitions—Necessity of an adjustment between the two countries——Principles on which it should be founded.

§ III. Commerce.

THE difcuffion of this divifion of our fubject requires little delay, and it will neceffarily be more concife than any of the preceding fections. The reafons of this are obvious—Commerce, or the trade of import and export, is not in itfelf fo much the fource of employment as the effect. Wherever a people are employed, either in raifing rude produce, or in converting fuch produce into manufactures, an export of their fuperfluities, and an import of the objects of their wants, will take place, and be proportioned to the amount of the numbers employed, and the extent of their employment. A number of fhips reforting to a harbour, will not neceffarily eftablifh either flourifhing manufactures or a fuperfluity of rude produce for export in its vicinity; but the eftablifhment of flourifhing manufactures will neceffarily attract veffels from different quarters of the world, and create a trade of export and import. Commerce † is not the parent, but the offspring of employment. Holland is in ſome degree an exception to this maxim; her carrying trade is a principal ſource of employment to her natives; but one ſingular example does not invalidate the general juſtice of the concluſion. Beſides, it may be otherwiſe accounted for on other principles.

But does not the exportation and importation of a country afford immediate employment to numbers, who navigate the neceſſary veſſels; and ſhould it not, therefore, be confined as much as poſſible to the inhabitants of our own iſland? The buſineſs of exporting and importing undoubtedly does afford employment to many naval hands; but the capital neceſſary to it employs a more inconſiderable number of people, than capital to the ſame amount in almoſt any other branch of buſineſs. This will be evident from

† It will be obſerved that I take commerce in the confined ſenſe of a mere trade of export and import.—It has been uſed in a more extended and comprehenſive ſignification.

from a ftriking example. A veffel which originally cofts a thoufand pounds, and requires befides a confiderable yearly fum to fupply her wear and tear, &c. will be eafily navigated by half a dozen feamen. They are the only people to whom fuch fums give immediate employment. But capital to the fame amount, employed annually in agriculture or manufactures, will give employment to hundreds. Befides,

The money employed folely in the carrying trade affords fmaller returns, and tends lefs to augment the capital, and confequently the employment of a people, than in any other bufinefs, perhaps, whatever. Hence thofe nations which poffefs a profufion of wealth, and who are, confequently, content with fmall profits, are they who engrofs the greateft part of this bufinefs. Such are the Dutch and Englifh; and hence we are to conclude, with Smith, " That the carrying trade is the natural effect " and fymptom of great national wealth, but " does not feem to be the natural caufe of it;

" it; and thoſe ſtateſmen who have been diſ-
" poſed to favour it with particular encourage-
" ments, ſeem to have miſtaken the effect and
" ſymptom for the cauſe."

It is folly, therefore, to lament that Ireland poſſeſſes ſo little of her own carrying trade; or to recommend any regulations which would force it into the hands of her natives. Want of capital, I muſt again repeat it, is her principal deficiency. If we can get our goods tranſported by foreigners at an eaſy rate, and at the ſame time employ our capital in other branches of occupation, which will afford greater returns, and greater employment than the carrying trade; it is better perſevere in the ſame plan, until our capital is ſo abundant as naturally to diſgorge itſelf, as Smith expreſſes it, into this channel, than prematurely to force what little wealth we do poſſeſs into a comparatively diſadvantageous occupation. By the conſtruction of the celebrated bill paſſed in 1782, commonly called "Mr. Yelverton's bill," the Engliſh navigation act is ſo far adopted, that

that the carrying trade of Ireland is in a great meaſure confined to Great Britain and Ireland. While it is not entirely confined to the latter, little inconvenience can, in theſe reſpects, ariſe to Iriſh commerce. England affords us freight nearly as cheap as any other country could do, Holland excepted; and it is but juſt we ſhould give them this monopoly, as tending to ſupport the naval ſtrength, and, conſequently, the chief ſecurity of both iſlands.

The principal circumſtance in which the legiſlature of a country can advantageouſly interfere with reſpect to commerce, ſo as to promote the employment of the people, is the procuring as free admiſſion as poſſible for her produce and manufactures into foreign ports. To a conſiderable number of foreign markets Ireland enjoys as unreſtricted admittance as any other commercial ſtate. Among theſe may be numbered the Britiſh Weſt India Iſlands, and American Colonies, whoſe markets were fully opened to us by the ſettlement of 1779; the United States of America, to which our exports

ports are confiderable, and daily increafing; Portugal, with which our trade is peculiarly advantageous; Spain, with which our connection is rapidly extending; France, Holland, Norway, Sweden, and all the ports of the Baltic.

The country into whofe ports admittance for all our manufactured produce, linen only excepted, is moft difficult, and nearly, indeed, prohibited, is Great Britain. It was to effect a mutual fettlement in this point that the celebrated Commercial Propofitions were principally introduced. It is not our intention to enter into a minute difcuffion of the merits of thefe propofitions as finally adjufted in England. They no longer engage the attention of the public, and thofe defirous of more particular information refpecting them than can here be poffibly afforded, will be gratified in the perufal of the various publications refpecting them, which iffued from the prefs at the period of their introduction. We fhall here only offer a few general confiderations on the propriety

priety and advantages of finally adjusting the intercouse between the two countries, on liberal principles.

The British prohibitions against the import of the manufactures of Ireland, which still exist, as well as the restraints upon export to any country, which she successfully disengaged herself from in 1779, arose, in a great degree, from the system of colonization †, by which Ireland

† It is curious to discover, on retrospection, the sentiments of England respecting Ireland, previous to her emancipation.—A most extraordinary petition was at one time presented from Folkstone and Aldborough to the Parliament of England, stating, that they had suffered a singular grievance from Ireland, "by the Irish catching herrings at *Waterford* and "*Wexford*, sending them to the Streights, and thereby *forestalling* and ruining petitioners markets."—A bill which was passed in Ireland in 1759, for restraining the importation of damaged flour, was thrown out by the interest of a single miller at Chichester — Even the liberal Doctor Smith himself was not free from these prejudices: "As the woollen manufactures of "Ireland," says he, "are fully as much discouraged "as is consistent with *justice and fair dealing*, &c."

Ireland was governed till the laſt mentioned period. The principles of that ſyſtem were, to ſecure a complete monopoly in the purchaſe of all the rude produce of colonies, and a ſimilar monopoly of the colonial markets, for the ſale of domeſtic manufactures. The conceſſions of 1779, and the final ſettlement of the conſtitution in 1782, completely ſubverted this ſyſtem, and Ireland became free to export her manufactures to any part of Europe, and the New World, that would receive them. England, however, though ſhe could no longer reſtrain the exports of Ireland, could prevent the admiſſion of her fabrics into her own ports, and ſhe has done ſo. Whether it is expedient that the two countries ſhould remain upon this footing; and what, in caſe of a change, are the principles which ſhould regulate their mutual agreement, are the points which remain with us to inveſtigate.

A variety of political reaſons occur, which it would be invidious to recapitulate, and which ſtrongly demonſtrate the neceſſity of a more

ſtrict

ſtrict commercial union between the two countries. Even ſelf-intereſt ſhould prompt England, if any meaſure of this nature could ſerve and enrich Ireland, immediately to adopt it. The ſelfiſh, narrow, and illiberal ſpirit of commercial jealouſy, would have us believe that one country could only flouriſh in proportion as its neighbour became diſtreſſed. The very contrary is the fact. The rich are much better cuſtomers to a tradeſman than the poor.— It is exactly the ſame with nations. The more flouriſhing a country is, the greater will be its demand for the different productions in which thoſe of its vicinity excel. And the greater the riches of Ireland, the more conſiderable will be her conſumption of different articles, for which ſhe muſt always reſort to England. This is not only evident from reaſon, but evinced by experience. Our imports from England have been ever proportioned to our wealth and proſperity.

But the neceſſity of ſome regulation of intercourſe between the two kingdoms, different from

from that which at present obtains, is evident by the resolution of the British House of Commons 17th May 1782.

" Resolved, that it is *indispensible* to the in-
" terests and happiness of both kingdoms, that
" the connection between them should be esta-
" blished, by mutual consent, on a solid and
" permanent basis.——"

Mr. Orde, in introducing his propositions to the Irish House, mentioned that his idea with respect to a mutual settlement had been that of a mutual dereliction of all duties between the two countries. The more this subject is examined, the more evidently, I am convinced, will it appear, that this would be the most liberal and generally advantageous measure which could be pursued. I would, in this instance at least, consider both kingdoms as one, and would no more harrass with duties the intercourse between them than I would that between shire and shire, or county and county. The perfect freedom of internal commerce is of all advantages one of the moſt efficacious for promoting national wealth and proſperity; and, conſequently, general employment; and, by ſuch mutual freedom of intercourſe, both nations would unavoidably profit, and each reap advantages from the proſperity of the other.

If ſuch a total change of ſyſtem is impoſſible, as ſome would have us believe, the next moſt deſirable plan would be, to lower the duties where higheſt in each country to the amount of the loweſt paid on the importation of the ſame articles into the other. This would at leaſt be diminiſhing an evil; and this was the leading principle of the Commercial Propoſitions. Whether the conſtitutional defects diſcovered in them were ſuch as warranted their rejection, this is neither the time nor place to examine.

F I N I S.

www.ingramcontent.com/pod-product-compliance
Lightning Source LLC
Chambersburg PA
CBHW030856270326
41929CB00008B/451

* 9 7 8 3 7 4 4 7 3 4 8 1 3 *